How to Deal With Difficult People

How to Deal With Difficult People

Smart tactics for overcoming the problem people in your life

Gill Hasson

CAPSTONE
A Wiley Brand

This edition first published 2015
© 2015 Gill Hasson

Registered office
Capstone Publishing Ltd. (A Wiley Company), John Wiley & Sons Ltd, The Atrium, Southern Gate, Chichester, West Sussex, PO19 8SQ, United Kingdom

For details of our global editorial offices, for customer services and for information about how to apply for permission to reuse the copyright material in this book please see our website at www.wiley.com.

The right of the author to be identified as the author of this work has been asserted in accordance with the Copyright, Designs and Patents Act 1988.

Wiley publishes in a variety of print and electronic formats and by print-on-demand. Some material included with standard print versions of this book may not be included in e-books or in print-on-demand. If this book refers to media such as a CD or DVD that is not included in the version you purchased, you may download this material at http://booksupport.wiley.com. For more information about Wiley products, visit www.wiley.com.

Designations used by companies to distinguish their products are often claimed as trademarks. All brand names and product names used in this book and on its cover are trade names, service marks, trademarks or registered trademarks of their respective owners. The publisher and the book are not associated with any product or vendor mentioned in this book. None of the companies referenced within the book have endorsed the book.

Limit of Liability/Disclaimer of Warranty: While the publisher and author have used their best efforts in preparing this book, they make no representations or warranties with respect to the accuracy or completeness of the contents of this book and specifically disclaim any implied warranties of merchantability or fitness for a particular purpose. It is sold on the understanding that the publisher is not engaged in rendering professional services and neither the publisher nor the author shall be liable for damages arising herefrom. If professional advice or other expert assistance is required, the services of a competent professional should be sought.

Library of Congress Cataloging-in-Publication Data

Hasson, Gill.
How to deal with difficult people : smart tactics for overcoming the problem people in your life / Gill Hasson.
     pages cm
Includes index.
ISBN 978-0-85708-567-2 (paperback)
1. Interpersonal conflict. 2. Conflict management. 3. Interpersonal relations. 4. Interpersonal communication. I. Title.
BF637.I48.H384 2015
158.2–dc23   2014029780

A catalogue record for this book is available from the British Library.

ISBN 978-0-857-08567-2 (pbk) ISBN 978-0-857-08571-9 (ebk)
ISBN 978-0-857-08572-6 (ebk)

Cover design: Wiley
Set in 11.5/14.5pt Sabon LT Std by Laserwords Private Limited, Chennai, India.
Printed in Great Britain by TJ International Ltd, Padstow, Cornwall, UK

Contents

Introduction

Difficult people are everywhere.

Theodore Roosevelt once said, 'The single most important ingredient of success is knowing how to get along with people.'

Of course, Roosevelt never met that difficult person at work that you have to deal with every day, did he? And he certainly didn't have your in-laws.

When people are nice to you, you can't help but feel good and be nice back. But when they're difficult, you're bound to be unhappy about it and react badly.

Why do other people get to us so easily?

The reason our happiness and well-being depend so much on our relationships is because humans are social beings; we seek and enjoy the company of other people, in particular other people who are easy to get along with and whom we like.

In fact, most of us would rather experience an unpleasant event – watch our team lose, for example – with someone who shares our negative opinions about the team than experience a pleasant event – watching our team win – in the company of those who are disagreeable and difficult.

But some people know exactly how to be difficult. They're the people who bring you down with their negativity, criticism or anger. They refuse to cooperate. They're irritating, frustrating and often infuriating. And if you respond to someone else's difficult behaviour with anger and blame, withdrawal or compliance, you may end up feeling guilty, stressed or depressed.

What to do? One obvious solution is to calmly walk away from them. This is easier said than done. (But not impossible: see Chapter 8.) While you can always walk away from a rude shop assistant or hang up on an irritating sales call, it's not so easy to cut yourself off from a parent, sibling, partner, colleague or friend.

A more practical approach to dealing with them is to start by understanding how and why other people can be so difficult. Chapter 1 will help you do just that. You'll see that difficult behaviour occurs on a continuum. At one end of the scale, difficult behaviour can be overt (hostile and aggressive); at the other end, it can be passive (uninvolved and inactive).

In the middle of this continuum is behaviour in others that can be the most difficult to deal with: passive aggressive. It is covert (dishonest and manipulative). In Chapter 1, we'll explore these patterns of behaviour in more detail.

However, knowing and understanding what's wrong with someone's behaviour doesn't change it. The thing is you **can't** directly change other people's behaviour; the only thing you can change is how you respond and deal with it.

In Chapter 2, we will look at the different ways you may currently deal with difficult people and help you to understand why you react to them in the way you do.

We consider the expectations and beliefs you may have about the ways other people 'should' behave towards you. Perhaps you blame other people for **making** you respond or behave in particular ways.

You'll learn that other people can't **make** you do anything; they're not responsible for how you feel or respond. You are. So taking responsibility for your reactions to difficult people will help you better manage them. Why? Because if you can take responsibility for your responses then, like anything else that belongs to you, those responses are yours to manage: to influence and direct.

Having thought about how and why you and other people behave and respond to each other as you do, the next step is to learn skills, strategies and techniques to manage difficult people: to know what to say and what not to say. A good way to know what to say and what not to say to a difficult person is to start by listening to them. Really listening.

In Chapter 3, you'll learn what 'reflective listening' skills are and how to use them to your advantage. As well as learning how to listen to other people, you'll learn to 'read' other people; you'll learn how to actually 'see' what other people's motives and intentions are.

By this point in the book, you'll certainly be ready to get on with dealing with difficult people. In the past, you may have thought that there was only one or two ways to do this: either grit your teeth and hope that they'll stop being so difficult, that things will improve, or get the difficult person to see just how difficult they're being.

Both of these approaches are unlikely to fix the problem. In the case of gritting your teeth and hoping things will improve... they won't. In the case of getting them to see just how difficult they're being, that's unlikely too.

You need to deal with the difficult **behaviour** – not the person. Chapter 4 will really help you here. It explains how to deal with other people calmly, directly and honestly using assertiveness skills and techniques.

You'll learn that there are several aspects to being assertive. Being assertive means being honest, clear and specific about what you feel, want and don't want. You have to acknowledge and often clarify the other person's point of view. You'll need to negotiate, compromise and, when necessary, stand your ground. You need to be able to identify solutions and consequences for when the other person refuses to cooperate. You'll need to avoid 'losing it': accusing and blaming or insulting the other person when they're being difficult. Finally, you need to know how to come across with certainty and confidence.

Sound like there's a lot to learn? There is. But you don't have to learn it all at once. You don't have to put it all into practice at once either, in an encounter with a difficult person. The good news is that you only need to remember to focus on one or two assertiveness techniques at any one time to make progress.

In Part Two of this book, you can see how, in a range of situations with a range of difficult individuals, people have only needed to use a couple of assertive strategies and techniques each time to deal with a difficult person.

However, some people aren't just difficult, they're impossible! They drain you and can even destroy you. In order to preserve your physical and mental health, your stability and spirit, there is really only one thing for you to do: withdraw completely. Chapter 8 will explain how you can do this in the third and final part of the book.

So, as you can see, this book can help you to handle all kinds of people in all sorts of situations – to make your life less stressful and a lot easier.

Once you've read this book, you'll no longer feel that other people make you feel or behave one way or another. Instead, you'll feel that **you** are in control. You'll see that you can choose whether to tell other people what you think, how you feel and what you believe.

Even if an encounter with a difficult person doesn't turn out the way you hoped, you'll be less likely to feel guilty, angry or resentful, because you'll know to simply reflect on and identify what you would do differently next time, in a similar situation.

In short, *How to Deal With Difficult People* will help you to develop strategies to respond calmly, be able to confidently stand up to others and know when to walk away.

The result? Other people are more likely to treat you in the way you want: with respect.

PART ONE

Dealing With Difficult People

1
Difficult People and Their Difficult Behaviour

Who or what is a difficult person? It's anyone who leaves you feeling upset or let down, frustrated or angry, humiliated or confused, drained or despairing.

A difficult person can be someone who behaves in an exploitative or unethical manner; they may be someone who creates a sense of distrust because they avoid saying what they really think or feel.

A difficult person may be someone who refuses to cooperate with you. They may avoid taking responsibility and duck out of commitments.

A difficult person can also be someone who is negative and critical; they find fault easily without offering any constructive or helpful alternatives.

Whether it's a manager who keeps moving the goalposts, an uncooperative colleague or the difficult-to-please client, your negative friend, sarcastic brother-in-law, critical parent or the infuriating person at a call centre, they all have one thing in common: they can be difficult to deal with.

There are probably times when you wonder how an encounter can go awry so quickly; you start to doubt your own perceptions, feel thrown off balance by the other person and find yourself acting crazy when, actually, you're quite a nice person!

Is it you or is it the other person? It's not always easy to tell if someone is deliberately being difficult or if it's just you who is struggling to deal with that person.

You may have no trouble dealing with a hostile teenager but you have real difficulty with a colleague who finds fault in everything you do. Perhaps you find it easy to accept your sister's negativity (the rest of the family find her draining) but find a friend's inability to be enthusiastic about anything the most challenging.

What is difficult in one context may seem as nothing in another; an uncooperative colleague is a real struggle to deal with in a meeting, but one to one you find it quite easy to negotiate with him or her.

Sometimes, it's not clear what exactly it is you're having to deal with. For instance, although it's not pleasant, when someone is being openly aggressive and hostile, you know just what you're dealing with. Too often, though, someone else's difficult behaviour is difficult to identify; it's hard to nail down what exactly it is they're doing or saying that's so infuriating.

When does someone else's behaviour move from being irritating to infuriating? It can range from mild or transient to difficult behaviour that is significant and persistent.

Difficult behaviour occurs on a continuum. At one end of the scale, difficult behaviour can be overt (hostile and aggressive); at the other end, it can be passive (uninvolved and inactive).

In the middle of this continuum is behaviour in others that can be the most difficult to deal with: passive aggressive. It is covert – dishonest and manipulative.

Let's look at these patterns of behaviour in more detail.

Openly hostile, aggressive behaviour

Aggressive behaviour is the most overt, open type of difficult behaviour. At its most extreme, openly hostile, aggressive behaviour is harsh and forceful. It can be intimidating; when someone is being openly hostile, they may shout, swear and be abusive. They often overreact, even to things that have little or no consequence to them.

An openly hostile person may talk over and interrupt you or oppose you by dismissing your ideas and opinions. They are unable to compromise with you and frequently 'lose it'. He or she usually feels they have to prove things and push a point. They insist they are right. You are wrong. It's a 'my way or no way' approach.

They are domineering and controlling and view the world through a self-centred lens. The more self-centred they are, the more difficult they are. Their steamroller tactics can leave you feeling like you've been flattened!

Why do people behave like this?

When someone is behaving in an aggressive, hostile way, it's because they want to make sure that things happen the way they want them to happen. Sometimes, it's because their expectations have been thwarted and they are trying to claw back some control. Some people respond aggressively if they think they are being undermined or criticized; they may feel ignored, insecure, misunderstood, cheated or put upon. They may be feeling impatient, upset or just plain angry.

Anger and aggression

It's useful to understand the difference between anger and aggression. Anger is an emotional and physiological state; a person can get angry about something but not necessarily respond in an aggressive way. For example, a political situation could make someone so angry that they respond by donating money to support a related cause.

On the other hand, it's possible to be aggressive towards someone – by mugging them, for example – without being angry at that person.

Aggressive behaviour can be **instrumental** aggression or **impulsive** aggression.

When someone uses instrumental aggression, they are using their aggression as an instrument. They are using aggression in a calculating way to get what they want.

In contrast, when someone uses impulsive aggression, it's a reaction, a response to something that has happened to them. Impulsive aggression is an automatic response, an

---

emotion-driven reaction. It is aggression stemming from a feeling of anger.

A colleague who criticizes you in front of others is likely using instrumental aggression to obtain promotion at your expense; your wanting to thump him is impulsive aggression!

Disguised hostility: Passive aggressive behaviour

There's no mistaking openly hostile, aggressive behaviour; it's **direct** and in your face. Disguised hostility and passive aggressive behaviour, on the other hand, is an **indirect** expression of what a person does and doesn't want.

Passive aggressive behaviour can be one of the most difficult behaviours to deal with because it's expressed in obscure, underhand ways. The person may appear passive on the surface but is really acting out their resistance towards you in an indirect or hidden way.

When someone is behaving with disguised hostility, they don't reveal their true motives and you end up tying yourself in knots trying to work out what's going on. You may find yourself getting upset and angry but can't be entirely sure it is justified.

Rather than saying what they do or don't want, a person who uses disguised hostility puts up a passive resistance to your ideas and opinions, needs and expectations. In order to get their own way, they control situations and manipulate you without actually appearing to.

Passive aggressive verbal behaviour

Typically, when a person is being passive aggressive, they are ambiguous; they give mixed messages and are unclear about what they really mean. They may use sarcasm or veiled hostile joking and teasing, often followed by 'just kidding', and deny there's a problem. If you get upset or offended by what they say, they may accuse you of overreacting.

Rather than say what they feel or think, people who disguise their hostility usually mutter their dissent to themselves or use a non-verbal way of expressing their feelings, for example, by giving you the silent treatment, dirty looks or rolling their eyes.

A passive aggressive person is good at being a victim; unable or unwilling to look at their own part in a situation, they will go silent, sulk and be sullen in order to get attention or sympathy. If they can, they will find a way to blame others, avoid responsibility for their own feelings and emotions, which, in fact, they brought about by their own actions.

Passive aggressive actions and behaviour

When it comes to tasks at home or work, a person using disguised hostility may or may not appear cooperative but, either way, they'll do things to disrupt or sabotage a task, activity or project, often by creating confusion around the issue.

He or she may decline to contribute their ideas, but when your ideas and actions aren't successful they may respond with, 'I knew it wouldn't work.'

In order to resist doing what you ask them to do, these people will stall, turn up late, drag their heels and procrastinate. They will find excuses for delays and reasons for not doing something, invent difficulties or complications or 'forget' about what they were asked to do. They can be deliberately inefficient, doing something badly or leaving it incomplete.

When a person is using disguised hostility in a passive aggressive way, they may or may not be consciously aware of how manipulative and devious they're being. Whatever, you are left feeling confused, upset, offended or frustrated. You may even feel guilty; you think you've done something wrong, but you're not sure what.

Disguised hostility is a form of conflict that doesn't allow either of you to engage sensibly in the issues; it avoids the real issues.

Why do people behave like this?

People usually express their hostility and resentment in underhand ways because, for whatever reason, they feel unable to say directly what they really think, feel or want.

It's a dynamic born of fear of being controlled, fear of confrontation, hidden anger and an inability to deal straight with people.

They may lack the confidence to say what they do or don't want. If they've been discouraged or suffered in the past for openly expressing their feelings – anger, frustration or disappointment – they will use less detectable ways to say what they think and feel.

Whereas a passive person will simply accept the needs, feelings and opinions of others, a passive aggressive person is not happy to submit to others. But rather than assert themselves and stand up for themselves in direct, honest ways, they resort to underhand tactics to get what they want.

> **Almost all our faults are more pardonable than the methods we think up to hide them.**
> **La Rochefoucauld**

Typical passive aggressive types are people who come across as having a victim mentality or who are persistently negative.

The victim

This person imagines all slights against them – real or imagined – are intentional. They become upset at any hint of disapproval. They are sensitive to any indication that you don't like them or agree with them. You have to walk on eggshells around them in case you say or do the 'wrong' thing and they accuse you of disrespecting them.

Rejection or the expectation of it makes them hostile. Their reactive aggression is more likely to manifest in passive rather than overt aggression.

The victim looks for signs of being excluded, but the irony is that in time their victim mentality – their sensitivity and negativity – does, in fact, cause others to avoid them.

They may wallow in feelings of self-pity because they believe that everyone else gets all the breaks. Victims are, by nature, martyrs too. They need to let you know how much they are suffering; they seek sympathy or attention by feigning or exaggerating any difficulty or deprivation they are experiencing.

The negative person

Negative people often don't realize they're being difficult but they quickly get on other people's nerves with their tendency to see or anticipate bad results or undesirable outcomes, difficulties and problems. These people bring your mood down with their pessimism and general sense of distrust.

They may also be chronic worriers; what could be a minor problem for you and everyone else is a hopeless situation for them.

Some people are so entrenched in seeing the negative side of a situation that they leave no room for positive things to happen. Their negative attitudes and opinions can be contagious. They may dash your hopes and discourage your dreams. Negative people can undermine your potential with their negative opinion of what you are capable of achieving.

Beware: if you give in and let their negativity define you, you will morph into their version of who you 'really' are!

Passive behaviour

Passive behaviour happens when a person does not express their true thoughts, feelings, opinions or needs.

This can manifest itself in different ways. A passive person may be a people pleaser; rather than expressing what they really feel and want, they go along with what everyone else wants, seeking their approval, wanting to be liked and unable to turn down other people's demands.

Instead of voicing their own opinions, or making choices that will be controversial, unpopular or could hurt feelings, they wait for others to speak first and then agree with pretty much everything others say. They may be clingy and needy and lean on you more than they should.

People pleasers are often placatory: appeasing, pacifying and attempting to win others over. But their compliance can get irritating and difficult to deal with, especially when they overcommit themselves and let you down because they can't say no to someone or something else. In this way, they end up damaging relationships rather than strengthening them.

Passive behaviour, then, can manifest itself by doing whatever others want. But it can also be evidenced by non-participation – not taking part or not taking responsibility. Initially, you may find these people agreeable and easy to get along with, but it soon becomes clear that they are not contributing, engaging or taking responsibility. They rarely commit themselves or initiate activities, preferring instead to leave it to other people to get things going and make things happen. They avoid decisions, leaving you feeling frustrated at their inability to engage.

Passive verbal behaviour

Typically, you may hear passive people say things like: 'I don't know', 'I don't mind', 'It's up to you' or 'Whatever you think is best.' But these responses do not tell you what that person really feels, thinks, wants or doesn't want. And, because they are accepting and rarely disagree, you begin to doubt whether they mean it or even care.

You may notice that they rarely stand up for what is right or wrong, back you up or support you. They prefer to avoid friction of any kind.

Why do people behave like this?

A person may have developed a pattern of unassertive, passive behaviour as a response to parents, teachers, siblings or friends who were dominant and controlling or didn't allow the person, as they were growing up, to express their thoughts and feelings freely.

They may think that others will be hurt, angry or disappointed if they do not do what other people want. In fact, they may believe that they do not have the right to state their needs and opinions.

They may be afraid of displeasing others and of not being liked and want to protect their 'nice guy' or 'nice girl' image.

It may be that a person behaves in a passive way because they fear disapproval or derision from others for their decisions and opinions, so they hand over control and responsibility to others.

But a person may also behave in a passive way because they can't be bothered, they're not interested, don't care and simply have no desire to contribute and participate.

No doubt you have recognized someone you know in these descriptions of difficult people and their behaviour. We all know at least one person who leaves us feeling upset or let down, frustrated or angry, humiliated or confused, drained or despairing.

Understanding how and why someone else is being difficult can give you a better chance of dealing with them.

But just how much is it the other person? It's not always easy to tell if someone is deliberately being difficult or if it's just you who is struggling to deal with that person.

2
Is It You?

We've looked at how other people think and behave; now let's look at how you respond to other people.

Tick any of the statements below that apply to you.

❏ If another person thwarts my plans, I find myself thinking about how to get back at them.

❏ When I have to deal with a difficult person, I come away thinking about who won and who lost in the encounter.

❏ If someone hurts my feelings, I feel vulnerable and defenceless.

❏ I tend to feel helpless when a discussion or conversation doesn't turn out the way I expected it to.

❏ I sometimes envy others or even resent people who are persistent in getting what they want.

❏ When I am having a row or a disagreement with someone, it feels like they somehow turn everything round to be my fault.

❏ I usually give in to other people's needs and wishes, even though I don't really want to.

❑ I often get irritated when other people seem to get away with all sorts of bad behaviour.

❑ Other people often make plans without asking or including me.

❑ I get annoyed when other people are difficult; they are deliberately trying to wind me up.

❑ I often feel that others don't appreciate me.

❑ When someone else has opposed me, I see things in terms of who was right and who was wrong.

❑ If someone criticizes me, I feel got at.

❑ I often go along with what other people think or want, even if I don't agree.

❑ I find it difficult to move on from an encounter with a difficult person; I tend to keep going over who said what.

The more statements you ticked, the more likely it is that you see the world in terms of 'me versus them'. Often, you may see the difficulties and problems you experience with other people as 'not my fault, there's not much I can do – he/she did this to me.'

To a greater or lesser extent, you may believe that when someone else is being difficult they are deliberately setting out to thwart you – to be uncooperative, to oppose you or trip you up. You may feel powerless to do anything about it. Or rather, you may feel powerless to do anything constructive and effective about it.

And because you don't like feeling helpless it's easy to blame the other person for what's gone wrong.

The prima donna and her resentful sister

Take, for example, 32-year-old Danielle. Since she was a child, Danielle's older sister, Marie, has been indulged as the temperamental ballet dancer. Their parents have been lenient with Marie and yielded to her wishes and whims.

Their mother, Carol, could have been an accomplished dancer too, but – as Carol often tells people – she sacrificed her career to stay at home and bring up her children. Danielle is a dutiful daughter. To keep their mother happy, Danielle and her brother Luc phone or text her every day and visit for lunch most Sundays. Not Marie. She visits when it suits her and gets their father to run her around like a taxi driver. Their parents give Marie money and attend many of Marie's performances.

Marie gets stroppy and sulks if she doesn't get her own way. Danielle thinks her sister is needy, demanding and selfish. She finds it difficult to be nice when she sees Marie.

Of course, how you respond to someone who is being difficult depends on several things.

- **Who** it is. Is it someone you know well, a friend, family member or colleague? Is it someone who is always difficult with everyone and everything? Is he or she an authority figure? A parent, your manager, a dominant sibling or friend? Are they confusing or scaring you?
- **Why** they are being difficult; to undermine or embarrass you? Are they simply having a bad day? Is it someone who is always difficult with everyone and everything?

- **When** they are being difficult. Are you having a bad day? Were **you** already feeling stressed or vulnerable?
- **What** they are being difficult about. Is it something you thought had been resolved and agreed upon? Is it an issue of great importance or a trivial thing?
- **Where** they are being difficult; in front of others, for example. Or away from other people so you have no one to back you up or witness their behaviour.
- **How** you are feeling. Are you feeling tired or stressed? Do you lack the confidence to deal with him or her or are you unsure of your rights?

No matter who, what, why, where or when they are being difficult, if you are finding them difficult then they are going to be difficult for you to deal with. You could simply resign yourself to their behaviour or you could confront them, either in a direct way or in an indirect, underhand way. There are advantages and disadvantages to these three ways of responding.

Resigned, accepting responses

If, for example, someone is mean, nasty or unfair towards you, you may accept their behaviour or simply withdraw. Rather than say what you think and feel, want or don't want, in order to avoid confrontation, you stay quiet. You may go along with someone even if you do not agree with them. You don't stand up for what is right or wrong, or how you want to be treated.

Why would you respond like this? Like Danielle, you may think that others will be hurt, angry or disappointed if you stand up for yourself and challenge them. Perhaps you think they will reject you.

Resigning yourself to difficult people and accommodating them can lead them to disrespect you, take advantage or exclude you. However, this accommodating approach can be useful for a number of reasons:

- When it's more important to keep the relationship rather than argue the issue.
- You need to avoid physical harm from the other person.
- When the issue is more important to the other person than it is to you.
- You want to avoid an escalation of the situation.
- When it's better for the other person to do what they want and discover for themselves that they are wrong.
- When you realize you are wrong!

Indirectly confrontational, hostile responses

When you are accommodating towards a difficult person, you simply accept, uncomplainingly, their actions and behaviour.

On the other hand, if you are unhappy about or resent what someone else says or does but are reluctant to assert yourself, you may respond in avoidant, underhand ways. You may respond indirectly to someone else's difficult behaviour. You may, for example, sulk, be sarcastic, moan and complain about the person to other people.

Why would you respond like this? You might express your resentment in indirect ways because it would not be safe or acceptable to express your needs, opinions and feelings or would be considered rude or selfish. Perhaps you don't have the confidence to say what you really think or you don't have the confidence to deal with the consequences of saying what you think and feel.

Rather than be direct, you've found less detectable ways to express your resentment and dissatisfaction with the other person's difficult behaviour.

Although this avoidant approach does not really let others know what you honestly think and feel, want or don't want, it's useful if you want to:

- avoid an escalation of the situation
- avoid a full-on confrontation
- protect your interests
- protect yours or someone else's safety
- stall for time.

Direct, confrontational, hostile responses

A direct, confrontational response means being insistent and may involve being loud and forceful: shouting, swearing and attacking.

Why might you respond like this? It could be as a result of being undermined, ignored, misunderstood, cheated, put upon or humiliated over a long, or even short, period.

Often, other people's difficult behaviour can be the last straw – the last in a series of events that finally makes you feel that you cannot continue to accept a bad situation; for example, someone is often rude to you and you've let it go, but when they insult a member of your family it is the final straw. You snap.

Although an aggressive, confrontational approach can lead to an escalation of a difficult situation, it can be an effective response if you need to:

* take immediate control of the situation
* succeed in overpowering the other person
* outdo the other person and win
* make something happen quickly
* take quick, decisive action, e.g. to defend yourself.

Blaming other people

As you can see, there are advantages and disadvantages to responding in resigned, direct or indirectly confrontational ways. Too often, though, rather than take responsibility for responding in these ways, when you can't manage another person, you may justify what you said or did and defend yourself by blaming the other person, saying that their behaviour made you respond like you did: 'She made me say that' or 'He made me do that.'

When you have a difficult encounter with someone else and you feel hurt, embarrassed or angry, it's easy to feel that the other person is **making** you feel the way you do. In fact, this was Danielle's approach towards her family: they 'made' her feel irritated and resentful.

But blaming the other person for your responses undermines your ability to do anything about your situation. Why? Because if you really do feel it's their fault and that they provoked you, you are unlikely to look for a helpful solution. It's the other person's fault. There's nothing you can do about it.

In fact, if you can blame them for their behaviour then **you** don't have to change anything about yourself or the way you respond; it's the other person who needs to make the changes.

This can be seen as mistaken thinking. A maths and spelling analogy is useful here. Imagine you misspell a word or miscalculate a maths problem and get the wrong answer. Your mistaken thinking makes you believe you're correct, that you've come to the right conclusion or answer.

In the same way, your mistaken beliefs about how much power and control other people have over your responses and how little power you have gives you the wrong answers to difficult situations even though **you** think your thinking is logical and correct.

Is it you?

Even though it often seems that way, people cannot **make** you feel a particular way. Others do not cause your feelings and emotions – you cause them yourself. Here's how:

There are three aspects to an emotion:

- **Physical aspects:** The physical responses inside your body. For example, when you are scared, this may involve an increased heartbeat and shallow, heavy breathing.

- **Behavioural aspects:** What you do, the actions you take, how you behave. For example, fight or flight when you're feeling scared.
- **Cognitive aspects:** Your thoughts, beliefs and expectations. For example, thinking, 'I'm going to get hurt!' when you are feeling scared.

Any one aspect of an emotion affects another aspect. So how and what you think – what you believe or expect – about a person or event or situation directly influence **your feelings.**

Suppose, for example, you were given a parachute and were going to jump from a plane. How you thought about it – your beliefs, expectations and perceptions – would affect how you felt.

If you had chosen to go skydiving and were looking forward to it, you would probably feel excitement. On the other hand, if you were having to jump because the plane was in difficulty, your thoughts – your beliefs and expectations – would be filled with feelings of fear!

In the same way that skydiving can provoke thoughts and feelings, what others say and do may **provoke** feelings within you but they do not **cause** your feelings.

It's not what other people do that's the difficulty, **it's how you interpret it.** For example, if someone arrives late for an appointment and you feel that they aren't bothered that you've been kept waiting, you may feel hurt. If, instead, you feel that their being late has cut down the time you planned to spend on something purposeful and constructive, you may feel frustrated.

On the other hand, if your friend's lateness gave you half an hour of much-needed peace and quiet, you may be pleased they were delayed and feel grateful!

Are you aware of when you try to blame other people and situations? Taking responsibility for your responses to difficult people will help you better manage them. Why? Because if you can take responsibility for your responses, then, like anything else that belongs to you, those responses are yours to manage, to influence and direct.

Learnt helplessness

The theory of learnt helplessness suggests that if your experiences and interactions with other people or one particular person have turned out badly or negatively in the past, you may have learnt to become helpless when dealing with that person or other people.

You now believe (rightly or wrongly) that you have no control or are unable to influence or manage that person or people. This then becomes what is known as your 'explanatory style' – your way of explaining your interactions and the results of your interactions with other people.

The good news is that you can unlearn old beliefs and replace them with more positive ways of seeing things and explaining things. Understanding how and why you and other people behave in certain ways is the first step. Having positive expectations can also help – you can read more about positive expectations later in this chapter.

There is nothing either good or bad, but thinking makes it so.
William Shakespeare

Expectations, values and rights

We all have beliefs and expectations about the right and wrong way that others **ought** to behave towards us. When others fail to meet your expectations, you may feel disappointed, upset or resentful.

For example, Danielle expects her sister Marie to be less dependent on their parents. She believes Marie should take less and give more.

You may expect your friends, for example, to be loyal, honest and trustworthy. Or perhaps you expect them to be fun and interesting. You may expect your colleagues to be cooperative and supportive.

Your expectations underpin your ideas of what a good sister or brother should be, what a friend ought to be, how children and parents, colleagues etc. ought to interact with each other.

If these expectations are not fulfilled, you may be disappointed, upset or angry. If you internalize those feelings, you may respond in a passive, resigned way or in an indirectly confrontational, hostile way. On the other hand, if you externalize how you feel, you may respond in direct, aggressive ways. But you may also respond in a direct way that is honest and calm, in an assertive way. More about that later!

If you constantly have high expectations of how other people should behave and treat you, you are increasing the probability of being let down. On the other hand, if you have little in the way of expectations, it's likely that you'll be taken advantage of.

Our expectations tend to be more a matter of habit than conscious intention; most of the time, we are completely unaware of how our expectations can create all sorts of misunderstandings, conflict and resentment.

> Where is it written that others must act the way we want them to? It may be preferable, but not necessary.
> Albert Ellis

It's helpful to identify your expectations about how and in what ways you think other people 'should' behave. How to do that? Start by identifying your values. Your values are ways of behaving that you think are worthy and are important to you.

Read the list below and tick any values that you expect to see in other people.

- ❑ Affection
- ❑ Altruism
- ❑ Appreciation
- ❑ Clarity
- ❑ Commitment
- ❑ Compassion
- ❑ Consistency
- ❑ Cooperation
- ❑ Courtesy
- ❑ Decisiveness
- ❑ Determination
- ❑ Dignity
- ❑ Directness
- ❑ Discipline
- ❑ Discretion
- ❑ Duty
- ❑ Empathy
- ❑ Fairness
- ❑ Fidelity
- ❑ Generosity
- ❑ Gratitude
- ❑ Harmony
- ❑ Honesty
- ❑ Humility
- ❑ Independence

❏ Integrity
❏ Kindness
❏ Loyalty
❏ Obedience
❏ Open-mindedness
❏ Professionalism
❏ Punctuality
❏ Reliability
❏ Respect
❏ Self-control
❏ Sincerity
❏ Support
❏ Trust
❏ Truth
❏ Understanding

Now choose the five values that are most important to you.

Your main values guide the way you behave and interact with other people. Your values are the principles by which you live much of your life. Your values can also act as an anchor: they can be relied on to support and stabilize you.

Your values also reflect your expectations about the way other people 'should' behave. So if decisiveness and reliability are important to you, you will probably expect others to behave in the same way; to make clear decisions, be definite, resolute and determined, dependable and committed.

When other people don't behave in ways that reflect your values – when they don't behave in ways that you think are important – you may respond with disappointment, resignation, frustration or anger.

Problems occur if you expect a higher level of action or reaction than the other is either willing or capable of.

When they behave differently from how you expect, you may think, 'What's the matter with them? What are they thinking to behave like that and to do that?'

But other people may not have the same values as you. This is not a failing on their part; it is simply strength on yours. Don't judge them by the same standard. It would not be fair. Hold yourself to that standard, but adjust your expectations and be more flexible in your thinking.

Your expectations should be realistic; that is, they should be based on what is a real or practical way for someone to behave according to the context – the specific circumstances or situation and the people involved.

For example, although it may not be 'right', Marie's relationship and patterns of behaviour with her parents have, over the years, become set. Danielle can't change that. It would help Danielle if she were to adjust her expectations, to recognize and accept that this is their way of relating to each other. Danielle cannot change that, but she can change the way she thinks about it.

Rigid expectations can make you believe that things can't be 'right' unless people behave according to your expectations. But this makes your well-being dependent on their behaviour. You set yourself up for negative interpretations of what's happening and you're also placing the burden of your expectations on them, which then makes you the difficult person!

Once you become aware of unrealistic expectations, you are in a position to do something to free yourself from being dominated by them.

Positive expectations

How can you have realistic expectations of other people?

Having an open communication style will help; communicate – let people know your expectations. Then other people won't have to guess what your thoughts, ideas and opinions are. More about this in Chapter 3.

Having positive expectations, rather than 'high' expectations, is what really helps. High expectations lead to specific, narrow outcomes.

Positive expectations, on the other hand, mean that you are open and flexible about the outcomes of an interaction with someone else. It works by you expecting and actively looking for a positive aspect of the other person.

With positive expectations, you are not expecting any particular result or outcome and you are less likely to feel thwarted, resentful, irritated and so on because you are not hanging your expectation on anything or anyone specifically. Instead, your expectation is for an overall positivity.

Imagine what would happen if you developed the habit of having positive expectations for your friends, family, colleagues and others you encountered.

Imagine if, for example, Danielle recognized that her parents actually enjoyed indulging Marie – that they didn't resent Marie. If Danielle had positive expectations, she would simply expect Marie to continue providing pleasure for her parents.

Try to avoid high expectations and stay in a place of positive expectation with other people. It's a powerful way to change the way you think about difficult people.

Beginner's mind

When someone else is being difficult, yet again, you probably come to your usual conclusions. For example, with a critical family member, you may think, 'Here she goes again. She's always like this: critical and demanding.' You fall into the same old patterns of responding.

The problem is, dismissing the other person's behaviour in this way undermines your ability to manage the situation. Instead of writing the other person off as difficult, try embracing a concept known as 'beginner's mind'.

Having a 'beginner's mind' means that rather than respond to someone in the same old ways – ways from the past – you put aside the beliefs and the conclusions you came to on previous times and open yourself to new possibilities.

For example, suppose you have to spend time with a person you have always found difficult to get on with. Imagine if you met them for the first time in different circumstances. You would know nothing about them so you would have no preconceived ideas and no expectations.

Next time you're with someone you've always found difficult to deal with, start with a positive expectation rather than respond to them in a way that's based on past history between you.

Responding to people in the same old ways keeps you out of the present and living in the past. It doesn't allow you to be aware of any new insights. Beginner's mind, on the other hand, allows you to take a fresh approach.

Begin again: Change how you respond to other people

Read what happened when Danielle changed the way she interacted with her family. It's a bit extreme, but it shows what can happen if you change established ways of responding to other people.

The resentful sister changes her approach

Day one
Usually, I ring my mother every day. Today, I don't. It feels odd.

Days two to four
I still haven't phoned my parents. Do they even care? Begin to think I may have been helping my mother to be needy.

Day five
Marie rings me. She's upset. A ballet performance she was rehearsing has been cancelled. Instead of trying to soothe her, I say, 'What a catastrophe! Ballet is all you know. Do you think you might never work again? Are you too old now?' She stops crying, gets angry and hangs up. My mother rings me. She has heard from my sister. What's the matter with me? How could I be so insensitive? I put the phone down on her. I feel scared and powerful at the same time!

Day six
I decide not to turn up for Sunday lunch. I don't let them know I'm not coming, I just don't turn up. My father rings me. He reasons with me. 'You're upsetting your mother.' I say, 'I'm sorry Mum's upset. What about you, Dad? Wouldn't you rather give lunch a miss and play golf?' This is a first, too, asking my father what he thinks. He is thrown. He says, 'That's not the point,' but I can tell it's given him something to think about. Maybe he'll rebel too!

Day seven

My mother phones. She says, 'I'm worried about you. Are you OK?' I can't remember her having shown any concern before. I become tearful. Mum says, 'You don't have to come round every Sunday, you know.' I'm amazed. She's quite nice really!

It's easy to get into established patterns of relating to other people; we co-construct how we behave with each other. A beginner's mind enables you to do things differently. Even a small change may make a big difference.

Be careful, though. Be prepared for people to get upset, angry or defensive. Think through the likely consequences! If you do decide to do things differently and change your behaviour, be consistent. Be prepared to be flexible, too, but don't give in.

Your personal rights

You know, of course, that you have legal rights. These are what you are entitled to according to the law. Your consumer rights, for example, legally protect you from being stuck with faulty goods.

Personal rights are what **you** perceive to be the correct, just or appropriate way to be treated. Personal rights are what you believe you are entitled to. And when you stand up for your rights, they can protect you from ill treatment by other people.

Your rights are reflected in your values; your values will inform your rights. For example, if you value truth, you may feel that you have a right to ask or even demand that others be honest with you.

If you value confidentiality, for example, you probably feel that it is your right to expect others to be trustworthy and to keep to themselves information you have given them about yourself.

Whatever rights you identify as being important to you, ask yourself, 'Do I think these rights extend to other people?' For example, if you value forgiveness – if you think others should forgive you for your mistakes – then, hopefully, you think it's important to recognize that other people make mistakes too and that you don't need to hold it against them!

Identifying your personal rights can help you to be clear about your values and expectations.

What rights do you feel entitled to?

❑ To say what I think and feel.
❑ To ask for what I want or need.
❑ To make my own choices.
❑ To make my own decisions.
❑ To change my mind.
❑ To make mistakes.
❑ To be successful.
❑ To stick to my values.

- ❑ To determine my priorities.
- ❑ To say 'I don't know' or 'I don't understand'.
- ❑ To ask for information.
- ❑ To expect privacy.
- ❑ To be independent.
- ❑ To withdraw and not be involved.
- ❑ To say what I think and feel.
- ❑ To refuse to help.
- ❑ Not to be responsible for others' behaviour, actions, feelings or problems.
- ❑ To be happy.
- ❑ To expect honesty from others.

What rights would you add to this list? Do the rights you choose for yourself apply equally to other people? Be aware that someone else's personal rights will be based on **their** experiences and expectations, so they may well be different from yours.

Values and personal rights are subjective – they are based on **your** experience and expectations of yourself and others. Only you can stand up for your rights; other people have a right **not** to respect your rights! However, when you are more aware of your rights, you'll be more able to set limits and feel entitled to defend yourself from exploitation, attack and hostility.

Once you are aware of and take responsibility for your values, rights and expectations, you will be clearer about what is and isn't important to you, what you will or will not accept, what your limits are and how flexible you are prepared to be.

That's all well and good, you may think, but I don't have the **confidence** to tell people what I will and won't accept, what my limits are and how I want to be treated!

The role of self-esteem and confidence

This is completely understandable. Of course, you need confidence to tell other people what you think and how you want to be treated, to say what you do or do not want.

Confidence is what you believe you can or can't do. So, in order to deal with difficult people you need to **believe** you can deal with them.

You've probably noticed that some people find it easy to deal with difficult people; they seem to have no problem in calmly standing up for themselves. They do not let a fear of confrontation silence them; they are prepared to take the consequences of dealing with difficult people.

They don't try to prove anything, but neither do they allow themselves to be mistreated.

People who are confident in their ability to deal with other people in a constructive way do not try to control what other people think and say; they are open to other people's views even when those views are different from their own.

Even if a confident person feels anxious about dealing with difficult people, they don't let fear and anxiety paralyse them: they deal with other people and situations **despite** their fears or worries. They recognize they have to start somewhere, however apprehensive they are.

What they have, and you can have too, is courage, the quality of mind or spirit that enables you to face difficulty despite your fear and concerns.

This is where your values, rights and positive expectations can be helpful – they can give you the courage of your convictions and help you to act in accordance with your values.

Confidence and courage come through **acting** as if you are unafraid, even (and especially) when you are.

So how can you be courageous and see yourself as someone who can manage difficult people and situations?

Building courage and confidence

One way to help build your confidence about your ability to deal with difficult people is to remember past successes. Think about occasions when you have been successful in managing difficult people. Maybe you resolved a dispute over a bill or an invoice. Perhaps you once acted as mediator between two other people who had fallen out. Or you successfully negotiated with a colleague about who would take on a particular piece of work.

Picture what happened, where you were, what you did, what other people's reactions were. What was it you did that contributed to a successful outcome?

Next, think of a situation where you want to ask someone to do or not do something or something you want to do or not do that won't require a huge amount of courage and confidence. Start small. Starting small means starting by saying something to someone that induces less fear and requires a small amount of courage to accomplish.

Learning to have confidence takes practice. You need to see confidence as a process, not an achievement to be completed; having confidence isn't a finish line you cross once, and the process won't always move forward. Take a deep breath, remember the successes you've already had and resolve to keep going.

Don't be afraid of your fears. They're not there to scare you. They're there to let you know that something is worth it. C. JoyBell C.

Having read this chapter, you've probably realized that to deal with difficult people constructively and effectively depends, to a large extent, on having the right frame of mind. Rather than see yourself as a victim of other people's difficult behaviour, if you take responsibility for your expectations and responses, then, like anything else that belongs to you, those expectations and responses are yours to manage, to use as **you** want.

3
Communicating With Difficult People

Courage is what it takes to stand up and speak; courage is also what it takes to sit down and listen.
Winston Churchill

Having thought about how you currently respond to other people, your expectations and beliefs about the way others should behave towards you, the next step in dealing with difficult people is to improve your communication skills, to know what to say and what not to say.

Knowing the right thing to say isn't always easy, particularly in difficult, awkward or heated situations. But communication is more than what you say; communication is a two-way process. It involves talking **and** listening.

Knowing the right thing to say is a lot easier if you first know how to listen. If you listen well then you are more likely to respond in a constructive, effective way.

Often, when people talk with each other, they don't really listen; they make assumptions and misinterpret each other, especially if the issue is contentious or complicated.

Expectations and assumptions can distort what you think the other person has said. Sometimes, you assume you know what they're going to say next, or you think you won't get your chance to say what you want to, so you interrupt and jump in with your response.

Other times, you may not understand what the other person is talking about; you're confused. Instead of listening closely, you're a few seconds behind, trying to make sense of what the other person has said.

And of course, there are times when it's tempting to tune out, particularly if the other person is moaning and whinging or is openly hostile and aggressive. Tuning out rarely stops them, though. If anything, they'll complain or argue more forcefully because they can tell you're not listening and not taking them seriously.

> Listening looks simple but it's not easy. Every head is a world.
> Cuban proverb

Active listening

The good news is that there's a simple and effective technique that you can learn. It's called 'active listening' and it's effective in two ways. First, active listening helps you to be clear about what the other person is saying. Second, because you have a better understanding of the other person's perspective, active listening helps you to deal with them more effectively. Active listening closes the loop in communication gaps and so minimizes the likelihood of communication breakdowns.

It is called **active** listening because you are active in the process of listening; you participate and make an effort to understand what the other person is saying and why they are saying it. It means concentrating on what they're saying, making sense and being clear about what they really mean. It's a simple technique but you need to practise!

Minimal encouragers

The most obvious and natural way that you usually show that you are listening is by using non-verbal communication to acknowledge what someone else is saying, making eye contact, for example, nodding your head in acknowledgement or shaking your head in disagreement.

These little signals are known as 'minimal encouragers'. Minimal encouragers are simple, direct ways to let the other person know you **are** listening. Sounds and words like 'uh-huh', 'yes', 'oh', 'mmm' and little actions like nodding in the appropriate places show that you are listening. With little in the way of interruption by you, minimal encouragers encourage the other person to talk.

When you are dealing with a difficult person, the trick is to use minimal encouragers calmly and in a neutral way, rather than, for example, a sarcastic or angry way.

Reflective listening

This is the key skill used in active listening. It shows the extent to which you've understood the other person.

It's a simple technique but it requires you to concentrate and focus. You have to work at it. There are three aspects to reflective listening: repeating, summarizing and paraphrasing.

Repeating

When you are repeating, you are simply saying **exactly** what the other person has just said. For example, 'You think that I've been harsh?' or 'You **weren't** calling me stupid?'

All you are doing is repeating what you've heard to make sure you heard it correctly. This is exactly the same as when someone gives you directions on how to get to another part of town or tells you a phone number: you are simply repeating the directions or the numbers back to the other person so that they can confirm you've understood correctly.

And, just like when you repeat directions or a phone number, you are not required to agree with what the other person has said. You just confirm that you've listened and understood.

Summarizing

This involves briefly and concisely summing up what the other person has said, the main points. For example, 'So, you're saying that first, Sam was only doing her job, that you think I came down too hard on her. Second, she's not said anything to you about it but you feel that you should defend her. Is that right?'

Paraphrasing

This is a restatement of what the other person has said as you understood it. For example, 'I think what you're saying is that I expect too much and that some members of the team are feeling that nothing they do is ever good enough. Is that right?'

Begin with a phrase such as:

- 'Let me see if I understand so far...'
- 'Am I right in thinking that you've said/you feel/you mean...'
- 'I think what you're saying is...'
- If you're confused, you could ask 'Are you saying ... or are you saying...?'

With both paraphrasing and summarizing, you express in your own words your understanding of what the other person said and you end by asking, 'Is that what you said?' or 'Is that right?'

Reflecting in this way gives the other person the opportunity to confirm that this *is* what they've said. It also allows them to refute or clarify what they've said. For example, you could say, 'It sounds like you're disappointed in me.' The other person can pause to think about it. They may then agree, that yes, they are disappointed, or no, they're not disappointed: they're actually very upset!

It's worth noting that there are benefits to overstating or understating a reflection; either one may cause a person to clarify or reconsider. For example, if you overstated the fact that someone felt you didn't listen properly, in order to get them to clarify, you could overstate what they said by saying, 'You think I *always* interrupt and I *never* listen. Is that what you said?'

Of course, it would be quite odd to summarize or paraphrase what someone said every time they spoke to you. The point is – and this is a crucial point – to listen **as if** you were going to reflect back. Whether you do so or not. This is why **reflective listening** is so powerful. It focuses your attention, stops you from interrupting, helps **you** to listen and be clear about what the other person is actually saying.

Reflective listening can close gaps in communication, minimizing assumptions and misinterpretations. Here's an example:

> **Lee:** I haven't got time to rewrite this report. I've already moved on to the next project. You seem to be making out I'm not doing my job properly. It's OK for you: you work from home half the week and your time is more flexible. I suppose that Bill has been getting on at you about the report again, has he? Well, let him stew. If I try to talk to him about it, he just doesn't listen. I bet you've been moaning together about me. I haven't got time for this.

> **May:** *Let me get this right; you think I'm being unfair and that I'm siding with Bill. You've moved on to the next project already and you haven't got time to go back to the report. Or did you mean you haven't got time to discuss this?*

This is not the first time that Lee has sounded off to May in this way; she's heard it several times before. It would be easy for May to respond either by switching off or by interrupting with her own opinions. Instead, by reflecting back, May shows that she **has** listened and tried to understand.

If you reflect back in this way – even though it's not easy if the other person is criticizing or accusing you of something – they are more likely to feel that their point has been heard so there's no need to repeat it. They are also less likely to continue to attack you or defend themselves.

The basic challenge in dealing with difficult people is to remain calm in a potentially highly charged situation. You have to get your own reactivity down.

Reflective listening slows down the exchanges between you. Reflective listening engages a part of the brain – the neocortex – that enables you to think rationally and reasonably. This is just what's needed in a potential conflict situation because it helps stop things escalating too quickly. Reflective listening enables you to understand what the other person is saying and to respond appropriately rather than participate in a downward-spiralling conversation.

When you communicate with difficult people by interrupting, defending or attacking what they say, you are simply reacting: responding in an opposing way. Reflective listening is a more constructive approach. It allows you to respond in a more favourable way, to set the pace and feel in control.

Seek first to understand, then to be understood.
Stephen Covey

Ask questions

Another advantage of reflective listening is that you are more likely to be aware of gaps in your understanding, so you are more likely to ask appropriate questions to help clarify your understanding.

In any situation where you need clarification or information, there are two types of questions: open questions and closed questions. Open questions usually begin with the words 'what', 'why', 'how', 'tell me', 'explain' and 'describe'. For example:

- 'What's the problem with...?'
- 'Tell me more about...'
- 'How did...?'
- 'Why do you think...?'

When you ask **open** questions, you encourage the other person to explain more. On the other hand, closed questions – such as 'Are you upset?' and 'Don't you want to do it?' – usually get a short response.

Open questions invite a person to express in their own words their ideas, thoughts, opinions and feelings. Closed questions give control to the person asking the questions. When you ask a closed question, it's likely that you will need to ask another question, and if you use too many closed questions, it'll be difficult to carry on a successful conversation.

Look at how the examples below compare open and closed questions. In each example, the topic is the same, but the responses will be different:

- Would you like things to be different?
- How would you like things to be different?
- Do you want to do this next?
- What do you want to do next?
- Shall I help you with...?
- How can I help you with...?
- Is it a problem?
- In what ways is this a problem?

When you ask open questions, though, do give the other person enough time to respond. They may need to think before they answer, so don't see a pause as an opportunity for you to jump in with your ideas and opinions.

Be sure that your questions don't come across as inter-rogative, attacking, defensive or rude; try to pose them in a calm, neutral manner. It's important to maintain a positive mindset when you deal with difficult people. Ask 'how' questions to get input, to get them to share responsibility for the conversation, for example, 'How would you like things to be different?'

Let the other person finish each point before you ask a new question. Interrupting is a waste of time. It can distract and frustrate him or her. But once they have replied, you may need to summarize or paraphrase their answer before you continue with your response.

Questions about feelings

Do ask questions in terms of feelings. Probably, you often ask, 'What do you think?' or 'What are you going to do?'

When it's relevant, ask, 'How do you **feel** about that?'

There is a difference in asking people how they feel over what they do and think, particularly when you are dealing with someone who is being difficult. Asking questions in term of feelings can give you an insight into why they could be talking or behaving in such an unpleasant or difficult way. A person often needs to have the issue and their feelings addressed in order to start interacting constructively.

In fact, what you are aiming for is to develop some degree of empathy, to understand the other person's feelings and point of view, to get an insight into where they are coming from.

When you empathize with someone, you do not have to sympathize, agree or let their feelings dominate yours. Your aim is simply to **understand** their perspective and feelings. You are then more likely to understand why you have a hard time with them and deal with them effectively.

Showing empathy

Ranjana, for example, is becoming increasingly irritated with her housemate Marcus. Marcus often moans and complains to Ranjana about his work, his colleagues and his manager. Ranjana finds his negativity draining and does her best to escape whenever Marcus starts talking about his job.

However, things change when Ranjana changes her approach. One evening, Marcus tells Ranjana about a meeting at work that day where they were told about forthcoming redundancies. Marcus thinks it's almost certain he will be made redundant. Instead of thinking about how she can shut him up or get away, Ranjana uses reflective listening to engage with Marcus. She summarizes what he has said and asks, 'How do you feel about it?' Marcus explains that he feels overwhelmed and uncertain about the future.

Ranjana may not have been faced with redundancy before, but she has experienced what Marcus is feeling – being overwhelmed and uncertain. Her interest and concern reduce the extent of Marcus's negativity. He feels acknowledged and therefore more ready to move on to discussing possible ways forward. Ranjana is surprised at how effective reflective listening can be!

So, be intentional with your listening. Remember, even if you do not reflect back to the other person, listen as if you were going to.

Successfully managing difficult people requires understanding that their feelings and perspectives may differ from your own. Active listening – reflecting, confirming and clarifying what the other person has said – not only helps you to see where they're coming from but also shows that you are making an effort to understand things from their perspective.

You do not have to make their situation your own, agree with them or let their feelings and opinions dominate yours. You are simply trying to narrow the gap between you both, to show that you are willing to try to understand the other person's situation, point of view, thoughts and feelings.

Identify and learn from good listeners

Can you think of someone you know who is good at managing difficult people? Do you think they are good listeners? How do they show they've taken on board what the other person is saying? What questions do they ask?

Practise active listening

Becoming a good listener takes time, patience and concentration. It also takes practice. But you don't need to wait for a difficult person or situation to practise active listening. You can practise with a friend. Here's how:

One of you talks for two minutes on one of the subjects listed below. When the speaker has finished speaking, the listener can reflect back what he or she thinks the speaker said and how they felt.

- a TV show or personality that irritates and annoys you
- a time when you were disappointed (e.g. you didn't get the job, house, flat or football score you wanted)
- the worst job or holiday you ever had
- a time when a friend let you down.

Non-verbal communication

There's a lot to be gained by developing your listening skills; it will help you to improve your understanding of other people's behaviour, motivations and point of view.

But it's not just what a person says – their verbal communication – that tells you what they're saying and where they're coming from. What a person does not say – their non-verbal communication – can give you a real insight into what's going on.

In interactions with other people where emotions and feelings are involved, research shows that communication is made up of 7% what is said, 38% tone of voice, 55% body language. This means that a huge amount – 93% – of how a person feels is communicated non-verbally.

The overwhelming meaning of a message, when communicating with others, comes from an unconscious display of the 'silent' language, which reinforces, detracts or contradicts what they are saying.

Often, you know what someone is feeling just by looking at their face; you don't need them to explain in words if they are experiencing one of the basic emotions: surprise, anger, joy, disgust, fear or sadness.

But it's not just facial expressions that can clue you in to how someone else is feeling. Other non-verbal communication signals – a person's gestures, posture, eye contact – can tell you a lot about their feelings, intentions and motivations.

Interestingly, when communication is difficult our body language becomes more pronounced. It doesn't take you long to notice that someone is angry if they are using short, sharp gestures. You can also tell that someone is anxious if they are fiddling and twiddling!

However, body language signals can often be hard to interpret. For example, it would be easy to conclude that someone crossing their arms is feeling defensive or someone drumming their fingers on the table is feeling impatient or irritated.

Certainly, someone crossing their arms could be feeling defensive – they could just as easily be feeling cold! And someone drumming their fingers on the table could simply be tapping out a rhythm.

You can't rely on a single gesture, facial expression and so on to tell you how they are feeling. You need to take into consideration a **combination**, or cluster, of non-verbal signals.

Clusters are when a number of non-verbal communications and actions occur close together and so indicate a consistent message. Clusters and combinations of non-verbal communications provide a much more reliable indication of what's going on than one or two isolated gestures or facial expressions. A single body language signal isn't as reliable as several signals, so do look out for a number of signs that all seem to add up to the person 'saying' one thing.

For example, you may notice someone has their arms crossed. Look again and you may see that they are not making eye contact and are talking in short, sharp sentences.

But if you notice they are stamping their feet, and when they uncross their arms they blow into their cupped hands, you will conclude that, in fact, they are cold!

Notice too, if what someone says matches or if it is at odds with their non-verbal behaviour. This is particularly important when it comes to dealing with difficult people who are passive aggressive and indirectly hostile because that incongruence confirms what you are already picking up: that they are not being honest with you.

For example, imagine you ask a friend whether they would come with you to collect some furniture you'd recently bought. They reply, 'Yeah, OK.'

You're not convinced that they really do want to help so you ask, 'Are you sure?' Your friend replies, 'I said "sure", didn't I?'

But the fact that they mumble their reply and don't make eye contact leaves you unsure. You may not know exactly what that is, but you've picked up the mismatch between verbal and non-verbal messages; you're sensing their reluctance because their verbal communication – what they say – does not match their non-verbal communication.

This mismatch is known as 'leakage'. Leakage occurs when a person says one thing but their body language, gestures and so on leak something different. It's unconscious; **they** won't be aware of it, but if **you** fail to recognize these clues, you risk being misled. You'll misunderstand what someone is really thinking and feeling.

So, when you feel that someone isn't coming across as honest or 'real' it's probably because their non-verbal communication doesn't match what they are saying. This mismatch creates a sense of confusion and distrust.

Understanding body language can be seen as a form of mind reading. If you can read someone's body language, you are reading their feelings and thoughts. In any one of us, whatever is happening on the inside can be reflected on the outside, even when we're silent.

So remember, when it comes to getting a better understanding of what someone is really feeling, you need to take a **combination** of non-verbal signals into consideration.

Intuition

Picking up on a combination of non-verbal signals in a particular situation can also be seen as your intuition. Intuition is an unconscious process of tuning in to and responding to a combination of non-verbal information in a specific context.

For example, imagine a parent is lecturing her teenage son about not having a party when she's away at the weekend. The parent finishes with, 'Did you hear what I just said?'

If her son vehemently replies: 'Of course, I did. I told you already, I'm going to Luke's house for the night,' it could put the parent on her guard. Why? Because when someone is being dishonest, they may overcompensate and the pitch and volume of their voice will rise. Combined with the lack of eye contact and crossed arms as he replies, the parent intuitively doesn't trust her son.

When people are lying, they may rehearse the words they use but not their body language. So when their body language says something different from their words, you know you're not getting the whole truth.

Look for the bigger picture as well as the details. Then, if you are in a situation where you don't believe what someone is saying, when it doesn't ring true or feel right, you will know it's because that particular combination of verbal, non-verbal and contextual cues doesn't add up.

Learn to 'read' other people

You can practise 'reading' other people. Turn off the sound on your TV. Watch people being interviewed on the news. Observe people interacting in dramas and soap operas. Be aware of the non-verbal communication, the gestures, facial expressions, tone of voice and so on. What conclusions do you draw from particular **combinations** of non-verbal communication?

Look for combinations that support your assumptions. If you decided that, for example, someone looks defensive, ask yourself why you think that. Is it because they have a glaring stare? Because their shoulders are hunched up?

Practising 'reading' other people and situations will help you to notice subtle cues during your own difficult exchanges and conversations, so you can react to situations more tactfully and effectively.

When you're waiting at the bus stop or queuing in the supermarket, use the time to do a bit of people watching. Observe people on a bus, train or in a café and watch how they act and react to each other. When you watch others, try to guess what they are saying or get a sense of what is going on between them. Are they relaxed, anxious, irritated? What does the way they hold themselves say about them? What about the way they talk? Does everything match up?

Speak fluent body language

What about your own body language? Does it help or hinder in a difficult situation? Mostly, you are probably unaware of how much you are conveying non-verbally, but even if you are silent you are still communicating through your posture and facial expressions.

Often, you can exacerbate a difficult situation without realizing it. Your body language and tone of voice can exaggerate, understate or contradict what you say. You may, for example, say sorry but your tone and body language could be communicating your frustration and annoyance.

Other people draw conclusions about your attitude and, when faced with mixed messages, either they focus on your non-verbal messages or your mixed messages create confusion and distrust in the other person. So aim to avoid sending mixed messages; make your words, gestures, facial expressions and tone match.

There's no need to adopt a range of poses, gestures and expressions that feel strange or unnatural to you. When you're dealing with a difficult person, you simply need to adopt a couple of confident-looking gestures or expressions and the rest of your body and mind will match up.

If you want to feel more capable and confident, and not just **appear** confident but genuinely feel confident, simply choose to do just two or three of these actions:

- stand or sit straight
- keep your head level
- relax your shoulders
- spread your weight evenly on both legs
- when you are sitting, keep your elbows on the arms of your chair (rather than tightly against your sides)
- make appropriate eye contact
- lower the pitch of your voice
- speak more slowly
- speak more quietly.

You can't control every aspect of your non-verbal communication; in fact, the harder you try, the more unnatural you will appear. But if you can just use one or two of those things consistently, your thoughts, feelings and the rest of your behaviour will follow.

It's a dynamic process where small changes in how you use your body can add up to a big change in how you feel, how you come across and how you deal with a difficult person.

Which two non-verbal behaviours would you feel comfortable using? Choose two and practise using them in a variety of situations.

Talking to difficult people

Understanding and managing difficult people isn't just about listening to them and knowing the right questions to ask. Situations like telling someone you are upset or angry with them, that you are not going to be treated badly by them or that their negativity is draining you all require that you know when and how to say so in honest and appropriate ways.

In the next chapter, we look at how assertive communication and behaviour can help you do this.

4
Standing Up to Difficult People

It takes a great deal of bravery to stand up to our enemies, but just as much to stand up to our friends.
J. K. Rowling

A demanding colleague who coerces you into doing things their way, a critical family member, your hostile teenager or annoying neighbour; whoever they are and however they're being difficult, you'll know that there's a number of ways that you can respond. And those ways are not always helpful!

Maybe you find it difficult to express yourself calmly. Or perhaps it's not easy to be open and honest. What to do? Learn to be more assertive. When you are more assertive, you'll be able to respond to other people without blaming, attacking or shrinking.

Assertiveness involves being able to say what you think and feel, need and want. You are able to stand up for yourself even if you feel anxious about doing so. You do not allow others to manipulate or undermine you; you assert your rights but you also take into consideration the rights, feelings and beliefs of other people. In fact, when you are assertive you encourage others to be open and honest about **their** views, feelings and needs. This helps both you and the person you're talking to develop understanding, trust and cooperation.

Being assertive involves initiation and action. It involves the ability to act with firmness and commitment but also to be open to negotiation and compromise. You know you have a choice about how to respond to others: no one 'makes' you do something or feel a particular way. And even if other people resent your determination and persistence, you are able to manage it.

You know that dealing with difficult people does not involve one of you being the winner and the other the loser.

How to be assertive

Being assertive includes:

- identifying and explaining the problem
- saying how you feel
- acknowledging your part in the situation
- saying what you do and don't want
- acknowledging the reply
- knowing how to stand your ground
- being able to negotiate and compromise
- identifying solutions, ways forward and consequences.

Identify and explain the problem

First, you need to identify for yourself and then say to the other person what exactly the problem is. Stick to just one issue; don't bring up a list of problems and issues.

Be clear and specific; hinting, rambling and making excuses can weaken your message or result in the other person misinterpreting what you really mean.

When you want to confront someone about an issue you can start by saying, 'I'd like to talk with you about ... what happens (or happened) when...'

Don't expect someone to be a mind reader and know why it's a problem for you. Tell them. There's no need to run off a long list of examples of past offences. Don't, though, take this as an opportunity to highlight the other person's every character flaw for the past two years. Focus on your specific concern and keep it brief, avoid going on and on long after you have made your point.

Say how you feel

Just as you can't expect the other person to know why you have a problem, don't expect the other person to know how you're feeling. Are you embarrassed, angry, confused or upset? If you choose to tell the other person how you're feeling, make sure you own your feelings. Don't tell them that they are making you feel like you do.

Simply say, 'I feel embarrassed/angry/confused/upset when...' Saying how you feel also shows that you are affected by the issue and therefore need to resolve it.

71

Of course, when you sound off by saying such things as 'What do you think you're doing?' or 'I don't understand you. You must be mad!' it's clear that you're upset or angry, but when you're confronting someone, they need to know immediately **why** you're angry. Confrontation needs clarity!

In the three examples below, you can see how the problem has been identified, an example given and feelings explained.

Example one

> *Duncan: I'd like to talk about what happens when I tell you about my work. Yesterday when we were talking about my promotion, you said, 'Well, that's about as far as I can see you going with that company – you don't have a degree so that's a reason not to promote you any further. I told you this would happen.' It felt negative and critical and I was upset.*

Example two

> *Fiona: Jo, I need to talk to you about our holiday. It seems you've changed your mind again about our plans. You first said you were going to drive, then last week you said you'd get the train and meet us both in Brighton. But Amy has just told me that you now want us to come over to Cambridge and collect you. I'm confused and feel frustrated.*

Example three

> *Mikel: Rita, we need to talk about how you manage employees in front of customers. Just now, I heard you have a go at James about the report he wrote. You were*

standing right next to two clients. They were clearly quite shocked to witness that. I'm concerned that it makes customers feel uncomfortable. It worries me that it looks unprofessional.

Acknowledge your part in the situation

Remember: other people do not necessarily have your standards and values so do not, at any point, say, 'There must be something wrong with you!' or 'Any decent person wouldn't do that!' Instead, if it's appropriate, you may want to acknowledge your part in the issue.

For example:

'I admit I talk about my work a lot.'
'I know I like plans to be definite.'
'I know I said I'd move James to another department.'

Say what you do or don't want

Next, you need to say what, exactly, you do or don't want to happen. If you don't say what you do or don't want, all you'll have done at this stage is dump your problem on the other person.

So Duncan, for example, may want his mum to stop being negative and critical when he talks to her about his job. Or he may simply want her not to mention again the fact that he dropped out of university.

Fiona may want Jo to go back to the original plan. She may want Jo to choose any plan and to stick to it.

Perhaps she would like Amy to pick up Jo and then both women collect Fiona on their way to the south coast.

Mikel may want Rita to stop being so rude and aggressive to other staff members. Or it may be that he just wants Rita to find somewhere private to admonish other staff members.

Who knows what Duncan, Fiona and Mikel want? Only they can decide what they want.

The same applies to you. Decide what you do or don't want and say it. Be specific, keep it short and concise. Your point will be lost if you ramble. Don't give lots of excuses; all you need is one genuine reason why you do or do not want to do something. Just say what you need to say then wait to see how the other person responds.

Acknowledge the reply

Once you have said what the problem is, how you feel and your part in it, you can just wait for the other person to respond, or you can ask, 'What do you think?' or 'How do you feel about it?'

Asking for their point of view or opinion shows that you are expressing your opinion and feelings about what you do or don't want, and not just making demands.

Use your listening skills here. Don't interrupt, defend or argue – just listen. Look like you're listening and show that you're listening. Before you respond, you may need to clarify what the other person has said. Remember, you do not have to agree with what they said, just be sure that you have understood.

Acknowledge what the other person has said. For example, if Duncan's mother had said, 'Well, it's true, you did throw away your chances when you dropped out of university – I'm not being negative or critical. Seems to me I can never say the right thing; you're so sensitive. Anyway, I imagine Oliver [Duncan's partner] agrees with me.'

Duncan acknowledges his mother's response by saying, 'I know you think I missed out on going to university and I know you think I'm oversensitive and you feel you can never say the right thing. I think...'

Be sure to acknowledge and respond only to what is relevant. In this case, what Oliver does or doesn't think is not relevant.

You may not agree with the difficult person's view but you've acknowledged that this is how they see it.

Be aware that being aggressive can get in the way of communicating what you are angry about. People stop listening to you and focus on your anger instead.

Ask questions if you need to clarify. For example, if Rita had said to Mikel, 'You try dealing with James then. He's a nightmare,' Mikel's reply could be, 'I understand that you don't find James easy, but I will not have you shouting at staff in that way. Are you saying you want me to speak to James?'

Acknowledging what the other person has said shows that you have listened and understood. It also gives them the opportunity to confirm, clarify or refute your understanding.

Try to keep your tone calm and neutral. Avoid whining or coming across as hostile in any way and notice if you interrupt. Catch yourself, and say, 'Oh, sorry – go ahead!' and let the other person finish.

Repeat the process. Listen to the other person's response and continue the process, listening, acknowledging and responding.

Know how to stand your ground

When people sidetrack you or bring up other issues, it's easy to get distracted and for the situation to escalate or spin off in another direction. If you get distracted, you are allowing the other person to control the conversation. If the other person doesn't seem to be listening, or tries to sidetrack you, you can avoid being distracted by sticking to your point. Repeat it calmly until you feel that you are being heard.

Don't back down, sulk or counter-attack. Rather than ignore their response or argue with them, calmly respond to the other person in a way that both acknowledges you have listened and confirms you are standing firm. For example:

> 'I know you said I'd regret not finishing university [*acknowledging what his mother said*] but could you please not mention it again?' [*sticking to what he wants*]
>
> 'I know you think I'm making a fuss [*acknowledging what Jo said*] but could you just stick to this plan now and not change your mind again?' [*sticking to what she wants*]

'You may think clients can't hear you [*acknowledging what Rita said*] but in future, if you have something to say to another staff member, could you talk to them privately and not in front of clients?' [*sticking to what he wants*]

Be able to negotiate and compromise

Where possible, aim to negotiate or compromise. Look for solutions and alternative courses of action.

For example, Duncan could suggest, 'How about I try not to talk about my work so often? And when I do, you be a bit more positive.'

With the changing travel arrangements. 'Is there anything I can do that could help you make a definite plan?'

And Mikel could say to Rita, 'Would it help if you let me know whether and when James isn't pulling his weight and then we could have a meeting – the three of us?'

Find common ground for a solution. Try to offer an alternative that works for you and benefits the other person as well.

Being prepared to negotiate means that you each recognize that any decisions or outcomes have been reached as a result of each of you stating your views and feelings.

Also, when you negotiate and compromise, you've neither given in to the other person nor got so het up that they can divert the issue by accusing you of losing your cool.

Meeting someone in the middle will always be the most constructive approach for conflict resolution, but if you do choose to negotiate or compromise, bend as far as you can, but no further. Know what your limits are and stand your ground.

Identify solutions, ways forward and consequences

By failing to prepare, you are preparing to fail.
Benjamin Franklin

When you know in advance that you are going to have a tricky encounter with a difficult person, you can think through how you are going to manage, what your limits are and how far you are prepared to bend.

It's helpful to ask yourself these questions:

- What do I want and not want?
- What do I want the other person to do or not do?
- What am I prepared to compromise on?
- How far will I negotiate: what are my limits?
- What will the solution, way forward and consequences be if the other person refuses to cooperate?

Having thought about what, exactly, you do or don't want and how far you're prepared to negotiate and compromise, you will need to decide what the solution will be if the other person digs their heels in and refuses to cooperate.

For example, before she spoke to Jo, Fiona could have thought through in advance what the solution would be if Jo did refuse to commit to a specific travel arrangement.

It's important to think in terms of solutions and consequences, not threats or punishments. Threats are a warning of trouble, a declaration of your intention to impose a punishment if someone refuses to cooperate. Threats raise the emotional temperature and usually lead to more conflict. Solutions, though, give you alternative ways forward if the other person won't cooperate.

And instead of thinking of ways you can get back or even punish the other person for refusing to cooperate, it's far better to think in terms of consequences. When you think in terms of consequences, you are identifying a logical result. Consequences follow naturally from the other person's action or inaction.

The consequences of Jo's indecisiveness and lack of cooperation were that Fiona made her own plans, plans that didn't depend on what Jo's plans were. She calmly explained this to Jo.

For Mikel, the solution was to support Rita by telling her to let him know if she was finding it difficult to deal with members of staff, so that they could meet together and discuss it. If Rita persisted in handling staff in such a negative way, the consequence would be that Rita would receive a warning.

You don't even have to tell the other person what the consequences will be if they don't cooperate with you. For example, Duncan resolved that if his mother continued to be so critical and negative about his career, the consequence would be that he would not visit his mother quite so often and only briefly talk about work. But he didn't tell her this. He didn't need to. Duncan just quietly cut down his visits and when she asked about his job he briefly replied and moved on to another subject.

But if you do explain what the consequences will be, take responsibility for the outcome: there may also be consequences for you. The other person may get upset or angry. The same reaction is possible if you choose to stand your ground: there may be fallout as a result. The other person may sulk, get angry or burst into tears. They may stop talking to you. If you stand your ground, you must accept that there may be consequences.

Often, an exchange with someone can go wrong without you expecting it to. You're unprepared and unable to think of solutions and consequences. Rather than make an emotional reaction and start issuing threats and warnings, calmly tell the other person, 'I need time to think this through.'

Thinking in terms of solutions and consequences is a powerful way to deal with difficult people because you engage the rational, reasonable side of your brain, rather than the emotional, impulsive part of your brain. Threats and punishments are usually the result of heightened emotions, and when you're reacting in an emotional way, it's difficult to think clearly, to be reasonable and rational.

Thinking of solutions, alternative courses of action and consequences gives **you** control and puts you in charge. You decide what changes you will make and what direction events are going to take if the other person doesn't cooperate.

So, slow down, think of potential solutions before responding and ask yourself: What's my best choice?

Building the confidence to be more assertive

Now that you've learnt the key techniques of what's involved in being assertive, we move on to other things that will help you to apply those techniques and be more assertive.

Start small

In order to build your courage and confidence, you can choose a low-risk opportunity to respond differently. It's best to start with something or someone fairly unimportant rather than with a situation or person you find particularly challenging.

Does someone sometimes snap at you? Speak up and say what you think or feel about it. Get used to telling it how you see it. Don't just automatically shrink or snap back. Calmly say, 'I wish you wouldn't snap at me.' If they respond with, 'I didn't snap at you,' simply respond by saying, 'OK.'

Once you feel comfortable in these low-risk situations, move on to other issues and situations.

Notice when you're best at being assertive. You may find that it's relatively easy to tell a friend you think their criticism is unfair. Perhaps you have no problem telling your teenager that you will not be spoken to in such a rude way and that if he wants to talk to come back when he's ready to do so calmly.

In tougher situations, with a hostile colleague or your demanding mother-in-law, for example, think to yourself,

'What would I say if this were one of my friends or my teenager talking to me like this?' For example, if your teenager shouted at you in front of others, what would you say or do? Can you replicate that response with your colleagues?

Where and when: Time and place

When you want to say something to someone who is probably going to be difficult, think whether you have to say something immediately, or do you need to wait until you are feeling calm and confident and the other person is more receptive?

It may not be appropriate to respond to someone else immediately, for example in front of other people or if one of you is very angry. In fact, when someone is angry it's easy for them to become irrational and unreasonable because the anger has overwhelmed the logical part of their brain. If either or both of you are very angry, you are both simply communicating with your emotions.

It's also harder to communicate clearly and effectively if you are stressed, tired or unwell. Sometimes it can be helpful to let people know how you are feeling, and perhaps to postpone a difficult discussion until a better time.

Although you may have to wait for an appropriate time and place, don't let things build up to such an extent that they just get worse. Tackle it as soon as possible. When you ignore difficult people, nothing will change. But when you refuse to indulge their behaviour, you encourage them to behave differently – at least with you.

Take responsibility for your opinions: Start with 'I' and not 'you'

A sure-fire way to get someone on the defensive is to start a sentence with the word 'you'.

* 'You always...!'
* 'You never...'
* 'You should...'

A sentence that starts with the word 'you' is probably going to involve an accusation against the other person that will alert them to become defensive.

'I' statements, on the other hand, will give the other person less to challenge: they can argue with you if you say, 'You always let me down...' but not with 'I always feel let down...'

If you tell someone, 'I feel let down', they can't actually argue with how **you** feel (even if they think you shouldn't feel like that!).

'I' statements such as 'I feel...', 'I think...' or 'I would like...' show that you are taking responsibility for your own feelings. If you were to say, 'You make me feel...', you are blaming the other person, making them responsible for how you feel.

Blaming someone else is not going to solve the problem, so take ownership of what you have to say and take responsibility for what you think or feel.

Sentences that begin with 'I' show that this is your perspective. For example, instead of saying, 'You really should...' you could say, 'I think it would be best if you...'

And instead of saying, 'You're wrong,' you could say, 'I don't agree with you' or 'I don't think that's right.'

You can also put it this way: 'When you ..., I feel...'

When you disagree, try to say so without putting down the other person's point of view. Suggesting that someone is wrong or bad or **should** do something will create resentment and resistance rather than understanding and cooperation.

Basic assertions and useful opening phrases

All of the statements below are **basic assertions**: short statements that communicate a quick 'no' or 'yes' to the other person.

- I've decided that...
- I need you to...
- I won't accept that.
- I don't think that was fair.
- I refuse to listen/to be talked to like that.
- I don't understand. Can you explain?
- Can you tell me more? I'm not sure what you mean.
- I don't have an answer to that.
- I'm not sure.
- That doesn't work for me.
- That's not what I want.
- I don't agree.
- I don't want to be involved.
- I'd rather not say.
- I want to do it this way/like this.
- No, I'm not comfortable with that.

- I'm not going to discuss it if you are going to speak to me like that/shout at me.
- I think it would be better to discuss this another time.

Say 'I won't' or 'I've decided not to', rather than 'I can't' or 'I shouldn't'. Saying 'I can't' or 'I shouldn't' implies that something is stopping you from doing something. Saying 'I won't' or 'I've decided not to' emphasizes that you have **chosen** not to do something – a choice has been made.

Actually use the word 'no' when declining rather than 'I don't really want to' or 'I don't really think that...'

Make sure your non-verbal gestures, facial expressions and tone of voice reflect and support what you say.

Keep calm: Avoid insults and abuse

If the other person won't cooperate or compromise, be aware that if you react by using abusive language or insulting them, either you give the other person a valid reason to withdraw or you hand them the ammunition to sling insults back at you.

You may also have given the other person enough counter-accusation material to divert you from the original issue; they may feel that the fact you became so aggressive is worse than what you've been upset with them about. Cursing and insulting may help you to vent your frustrations in the short term but not as much as actually pinpointing the problem and finding a solution will in the long term.

Challenge extreme terms

Often, when people are being difficult, they speak in extreme terms that match their worldviews.

So, if the other person says, 'I **always** have to' or 'You **never**...', acknowledge their view, but then present your perspective. 'I know you think I **never**... but actually, I often...' or, 'I understand that it seems like it's **always** you, and yet...'

See if you can avoid linking sentences with the word 'but'. When the other person hears 'but', they know you are going to refute their view. Try to avoid the word altogether or, when it's appropriate, use the word 'and' rather than 'but'. For example, 'I know you feel angry and I'm feeling upset.' Sounds so much less defensive than 'I know you're angry **but** I'm feeling upset.'

Another example of this is if you apologize for something: 'I'm sorry I raised my voice, but I couldn't help it.' The 'but' disqualifies the apology. Take responsibility for shouting.

Rehearse

You can try out assertive responses in front of a mirror, or get a friend to give you feedback and suggestions. If you know that you are going to be in a situation – a meeting at work or a family meeting – where your ideas or opinions are often ignored, rehearse the situation with someone else.

Rehearse not just **what** you're going to say but also how you're going to **feel**. You may well feel apprehensive or even scared. Seeing yourself looking calm, having one clear message and being firm but fair will create a clear behavioural blueprint for your mind.

Maintain your composure: Use confident body language

Rehearse your delivery showing open, calm body language. How you stand or sit, the gestures you use, how you look at someone and use your voice are all very important. They help convey how you see yourself in relation to the person you are talking to.

When a difficult person irritates or annoys you, it becomes obvious to the other person through your tone of voice and your body language. This only fuels an already difficult situation.

Think about what your body language reveals regarding your respect – or lack of respect – for the other person. Refrain from behaviour that could escalate the situation, such as rolling your eyes, pursing your lips or shaking your head.

And, of course, be aware that if you are hunched up, speak hesitantly and avoid eye contact, you are not coming across as confident and convincing.

In Chapter 3 you will have read that if you want to feel calm and confident, you only need to adopt a couple of confident body language gestures, postures or ways of using your voice to have an impact on how you feel, how you behave and the impact you have on other people.

Self-control is critical in dealing with people who are challenging or difficult. Losing control = losing. Remember that staying calm increases your effectiveness and ability to think calmly.

Choosing how to respond

Some situations start with a power imbalance; if the difficult person is a tutor, manager or older family member, for example, even the most assertive people can feel intimidated and struggle to deal with that person. But whoever they are, other people are human beings like you, and the principles of mutual respect should still apply.

How you respond to a difficult person can depend on who it is and the context in which the exchange takes place. You don't have to be assertive – it's a choice. You can choose whether to tell other people what you think, how you feel and what you believe.

Sometimes a more aggressive approach **may** be more appropriate, if you need to take immediate control of the situation, for example. At other times, a passive approach may be appropriate, for example when you want to avoid an escalation of the situation or avoid any friction and conflict.

How do you know whether you should assert yourself? If the situation allows you to think about it, consider whether you'll regret it if you are not assertive in this situation; what's at stake? What have you got to gain or lose?

What are the probable consequences of your possible assertion? Could asserting yourself make things worse?

You may think that if you choose to submit to or withdraw from a situation you are being weak and powerless, or that you will lose the respect of others. This does not have to be the case. As long as you accept responsibility for how you choose to respond, do it with grace and goodwill and don't blame the other person for **making** you respond in an unassertive way, then you are in control.

Being assertive means being direct and honest. An Arab proverb says you must pass through three gates before you say anything: Is it necessary? Is it kind? Is it true?

What you say to a difficult person should be able to pass through at least two of these gates. So, telling your belligerent manager, for example, that he's got a face like a slapped arse may be true, but it will never pass the 'necessary' or 'kind' gates! Be honest and try your best to be considerate.

Although you are aiming to behave and communicate in a way that is fair both to you and to others, unfortunately, some people may find it easier to label **you** as difficult when you reach your limits and either stand firm or withdraw.

It is important not to give up if a situation doesn't turn out the way you hoped. Reflect on the conversation afterwards. Don't get angry and resentful – that will just prevent you from thinking clearly and constructively. Instead, ask yourself what you would do differently next time, in a similar situation. Even if you don't get the outcome you want, you will have the satisfaction of knowing that you handled the situation well.

Remember, you can only change **your** behaviour, not theirs, but if you behave and communicate assertively more consistently, other people are more likely to treat you in the way you want: with respect. Adopt the attitude, 'change begins with me.' By changing your approach you may find others respond differently to you.

As you can see, there're several aspects to being assertive. You need to be honest, clear and specific about what you feel, want and don't want. You have to acknowledge and, when necessary, clarify what the other person says and feels, be able to stand your ground and/or negotiate and compromise. You need to identify solutions and consequences.

However, it's not possible to do all these things at once. It would be impractical and weird to carry around a checklist to refer to every time you had an encounter with a difficult person. You've got to start somewhere, though. Set yourself up to succeed by choosing just one or two aspects of assertiveness to focus on using with someone else.

For example, the next time you are dealing with a difficult person, you could choose to just focus on listening to and acknowledging what the other person says. Or you may decide to make sure you say how you feel and start statements with 'I' and not 'you'.

In Part Two, you can see how, in a range of different scenarios, people have used different assertive strategies and techniques to deal with a range of difficult people.

PART TWO
Putting It Into Practice

5
Dealing With Direct Hostility

Who doesn't encounter difficult, hostile people every now and again? Whether it's someone in your family, at work or out in public, openly hostile people are confrontational, obnoxious and intimidating. An encounter with an openly hostile person can leave you feeling upset, powerless and angry.

People usually behave in this way for one of two reasons: to dominate, control and get what they want (instrumental aggression) or as a reaction, a response to something that has or hasn't happened to them (impulsive aggression).

When someone uses instrumental aggression, it's because they've learnt that by being difficult they can get whatever they want from another person. For them, their disagreeable ways – their aggression and hostility – are nothing more than a means to serve their ends. Yet, to you, their aggression is a weapon that leaves you feeling hurt, confused, perhaps even bullied.

When someone uses impulsive aggression it's usually as a result of an unmet expectation or need, and they now feel wronged or let down. Sometimes their anger may build; other times something suddenly happens which makes them angry, even enraged.

Whether someone is using instrumental aggression or is impulsively aggressive (the situations in this chapter are examples of both), it can be difficult to manage your own feelings. There are, though, ways to avoid reacting emotionally to someone else's hostility; you'll need to use listening skills and take an assertive approach.

You can choose whether to let the hostile person dictate to you what is going to be done. You can choose whether to engage. You can walk away at any point in the confrontation with a hostile person.

It's helpful to remind yourself whose problem this really is: the hostile person's, not yours. Only take responsibility for your own actions. You are not responsible for anyone else's behaviour or for the emotions someone else is feeling. You are not to blame if they choose to be angry or upset with you, someone or something else. They need to manage their own feelings and reactions.

With aggressive people you must send a clear signal that you are strong and capable – anything less is an invitation for further attacks.

You can, however, help or exacerbate the situation according to your responses.

If you step out boldly, you send out a quite different message, one of confidence.

Remember to use assertive body language; you may not be feeling very confident but you'll certainly look it. Remind yourself to use just two or three confident actions:

- stand or sit straight
- keep your head level
- relax your shoulders
- spread your weight evenly, on both legs
- If sitting, keep your elbows on the arms of your chair (rather than tightly against your sides)
- make appropriate eye contact
- lower the pitch of your voice
- speak more slowly.

If you can just use one or two of those things consistently, your thoughts, feelings and the rest of your behaviour will catch up. It's a dynamic process where small changes in how you use your body can add up to a big change in how you feel, how you behave and the impact you have on other people.

An aggressive manager

Ricardo works as a journalist for a local newspaper. He gets on quite well with his editor, Moira, but sometimes – particularly when she's stressed – Moira has an aggressive approach that Ricardo finds intimidating. Moira often demands rather than asks. She doesn't listen and interrupts others when they're talking.

Yesterday, she snapped at Ricardo that a feature he'd written was 'pointless' and 'badly written'. When Ricardo attempted to discuss it with her, she interrupted him and told him that he should either rewrite the feature or 'spike' it. She then went off to a meeting.

The difficulty

If you have someone like Moira in your life – a manager, colleague or family member – it's easy to feel demoralized and got at by their behaviour. We're not talking about someone who is a full-on bully here; this is more about someone who, in many ways, is a reasonable person. It's just that sometimes – maybe when they're stressed – their abrasiveness is difficult to deal with.

Their intimidating approach makes it unlikely that someone will have the courage to challenge them. But unless you challenge the other person, they are not going to change.

Of course, you need confidence to tell other people how you do or don't want them to behave towards you.

But rather than let fear and anxiety paralyse you, you need to deal with people like Moira **despite** your fears. You'll need courage to face them despite your fear and concerns.

Is it you?

It could be. Maybe they could be like this with anyone but you appear weaker than others around you and make it easy for someone like Moira to ignore, interrupt or criticize you.

You must not try to please or pacify them or ingratiate yourself with them, but you can't stay silent either.

Your aim

To say how you do and don't want to be treated.

What to do and say

1. Decide what the problem is

Is it that the other person has shouted at you? Is it that they have unfairly criticized you for something you've done? Perhaps they aren't listening to you. Do they keep interrupting? Before you say anything, be very clear with yourself what it is you don't like about the way they are behaving towards you. Set limits. What are you willing and unwilling to accept from someone else's behaviour?

Say what you do or don't want. Get used to telling it how you see it. If someone snaps at you, saying, for example, 'I've told you twice already!' don't just automatically shrink or attack. Calmly say, 'I'd rather you just told me again, instead of snapping at me.' If the other person responds with, 'Don't be ridiculous. I didn't snap at you,' simply respond by saying, 'I'm not being ridiculous. Could you just explain it again?' Or if someone were using sarcasm against you, you would respond with, 'Could you please just tell me what you want?'

If they interrupt you, wait until they finish and say, 'I'd like to finish what I was saying now.'

2. Start with 'I' not 'you'

A sure-fire way to get someone on the defensive is to start a sentence with the word 'you'.

'You always interrupt!' or 'You never listen!' A sentence that starts with the word 'you' is probably going to involve an accusation against the other person that will alert them to become defensive.

Blaming someone else is not going to solve the problem, so take responsibility for what you think or feel.

Avoid insults. Say how you feel and what you do or don't want without putting the other person down. Suggesting that someone is mad or bad will only provoke derision and resistance.

3. Choose where and when: Time and place

It may not be appropriate to respond to the other person immediately, for example in front of other people or if one of you is stressed. However, if you have to wait for an appropriate time and place, don't let things build up to such an extent that they just get worse. Tackle it as soon as possible.

4. Listen, respond briefly but stand your ground

For example, when Ricardo later told Moira, 'I didn't get a chance to discuss the feature in more detail. You went off before I could explain or ask you more about what exactly it was that you wanted.' Moira snapped back, 'Look, I told you what you'd written just wasn't right. I can't see what the problem is.' Ricardo replied, 'I know you said it wasn't right and you can't see what my problem is.' [*acknowledging what Moira said*] 'Please don't snap at me. Can we talk about it – now or later?' [*sticking to what he wants*]

Remember to keep your tone calm and neutral. Avoid whining or coming across as hostile in any way.

You may not get what you want every time, but don't let that deter you. If you consistently respond to someone in this assertive way then, more than likely, the message will get through.

Angry customer or client

Paul works on the reception desk of an adult education centre. Last week he was faced with an angry student, Veronica. She told Paul that she'd recently enrolled online on two courses: a French course and an IT course. When Veronica arrived for the French course, Paul's colleague could find no record of her enrolment – the course was now full and Veronica would not be able to join it. Veronica was disappointed.

The following week, Veronica arrived for the IT course, only to discover that it was cancelled. There weren't enough students to run the course. Paul's colleague had failed to let Veronica know in good time.

Veronica was now angry, telling Paul that the adult education centre was 'useless'. She demanded to know what Paul was going to do to rectify the situation.

The difficulty

When someone is angry, the anger has overtaken the rational, reasonable part of their mind. It's easy for them to become unreasonable and illogical. Their ability to think in a calm, reasonable way has been switched off. So, it's as if you are communicating with the emotion, not the person. In this situation, you can't tell the person (unless they are being abusive) to go away and come back when they're feeling calmer. You will probably have to deal with it there and then.

Is it you?

No. Unless you're the one responsible for the mistake. Even then, you cannot be responsible for how someone else feels – just as no one can make you feel a certain way. You also can't be responsible for how they respond.

Your aim

To listen to and acknowledge the other person's situation and feelings and offer a solution.

What to do and say

1. Use reflective listening

Reflective listening can defuse a situation like this. It helps the other person see that their feelings and point of view are being taken seriously. Reflective listening also helps you to manage the exchange.

An angry person needs to let it all out, so don't say anything until they've finished. Don't interrupt, defend yourself or disagree – if you do, you are just adding fuel to the fire.

Once they have finished speaking, acknowledge what they've said.

Here's how Paul handled it:

> **Veronica:** This is ridiculous. First, you don't have my enrolment then, when you do have my enrolment details, no one contacts me to let me know the course is cancelled. I've been let down twice. I could have signed up for the French class at another college but I've probably missed the closing date for that now. No one here seems to know what they're doing. What are you going to do about it? You're useless.

> **Paul:** *I understand that you're very disappointed and that we've let you down* [acknowledging what was said and how she feels]. *I'm sorry this has happened. What I suggest...*

> **Veronica:** [*interrupting Paul*] Yes. I am **very** disappointed. I feel very let down. So what are you going to do about it?

> **Paul:** *What I was going to say was that I could see what other days we have a French class that might suit you. Or–*

> **Veronica:** [*interrupting again*] I can only do Monday or Friday mornings.

> **Paul:** OK. *You're only free on those two mornings* [acknowledging what Veronica said]. *If* **we** *don't have anything on a Friday, I can phone the college on the other side of town and see what they have on a Monday or Friday.*

By using reflective listening in the same way that Paul has, you avoid being drawn into arguments and remain focused on the issue in hand by responding only to what is relevant and what you can or should deal with.

The conversation continued:

> **Veronica:** What about the IT class? I really need to get some IT skills and I was relying on getting on this course to help me. My friend Jamal has done this course. He said the tutor is really good. I enrolled online. What happened there? Why wasn't my registration processed?

> *Paul: OK, you still want to get onto an IT class. That's great to hear that someone else has recommended the course to you* [acknowledging]. *Let me sort out the French class first and we can move on to looking into IT classes. I'm not sure why your online enrolment failed* [acknowledging]. *If you enrol online in future, do make sure you receive a confirmation email. If you don't, you can phone us to check* [offering a solution].

2. Negotiate and offer compromises

Where possible, aim to negotiate and offer a compromise solution and alternative course of action. Paul has done this. Although it's difficult with someone who is rude, do refrain from making judgements. Paul, for example, did not say, 'You should have realized you didn't have a place when you didn't get a confirmation email. Anyone would know that.' Instead, he phrased it in more helpful way, saying, 'If you enrol online in future, do make sure you receive a confirmation email. If you don't, you can phone us to check.'

It's not the easiest approach, but responding to rudeness with a pleasant neutral attitude can help defuse the situation and give the other person a way to back down with grace. Being respectful and kind can also help you feel less stressed when you're faced with someone who is difficult to deal with.

Angry teenager

Mo's son, Jack, is 13. In recent months, Mo has battled with Jack about a variety of things which ended up with Jack flying off the handle, shouting and swearing at Mo. Yesterday, he had the following exchange with Jack:

Mo: I got a text from your history teacher. Why didn't you do your homework?

Jack: I just didn't. I'm fucking pissed off with that teacher.

Mo: Don't you dare talk like that!

Jack: Why not? You swear, too.

Mo: I'm warning you. You'd better change your attitude. And go and clean up your room.

As Jack storms off to his room, Mo says he's going to remove Jack's Xbox from his room for a week. He says, 'I warned you this would happen if you didn't do your homework again.' (Mo relents the next day and lets Jack keep his Xbox.)

Jack complains loudly and emotionally about how unfair Mo is. Before he slammed his bedroom door, Mo heard him mumble under his breath 'Stupid bastard.'

The difficulty

It's disturbing and upsetting when your young son or daughter turns into someone who is openly hostile.

If your teenager's behaviour and your reactions are well established, it won't be easy to break the cycle. But don't let this put you off. Rather than seeing things in terms of 'me versus you', you can use a 'beginner's mind': you can try a new, more constructive approach. It's never too late!

Is it you?

Yes. It is you. You are the parent and you are the adult. It's your job to take control. You don't have to put up with swearing but be careful how you react, because your response can either improve or weaken your relationship. Being too lenient could lead to more worrisome behaviour. Be too strict, though, and your teenager could feel that they can't express himself, which will lead to a communication shutdown.

Your aim

To say what is and isn't acceptable. To set limits and consequences and to stick to them.

What to do and say

1. Use reflective listening

You can help avoid a full-blown argument and manage the situation before it has a chance to get out of hand by using reflective listening. It will help to slow the situation down. Here's how Mo could start to handle the exchange:

> **Mo:** I've received a text from your history teacher. Why didn't you do your homework?

> *Jack: I just didn't. I'm fucking pissed off with that teacher.*

> **Mo:** You might feel strongly about your teacher [*acknowledging what Jack said*], but can you tell me why you didn't do your homework?

> *Jack: Because I just didn't. All right?*

> **Mo:** Fine. I can see you're angry [*acknowledging Jack's feelings*]. Let's talk about it later.

> *Jack: No, I'm not going to fucking talk about it later.*

At this point, saying anything more is likely to escalate the situation. When one or both of you are angry, the anger will overtake the rational, reasonable part of your mind and it's easy to become unreasonable and illogical. Either person's ability to think in a calm, reasonable way will have been overridden.

Here, Jack is already angry – Mo must keep **his** reaction as mild as possible. Yelling, making threats or shouting 'How dare you? I'm your father!' will only make things worse.

2. Choose the right time to discuss the situation

Later, when you are feeling calm and your teenager is likely to be more receptive, you need to talk. Negotiate. Be clever about it. If your teenager asks you for something – a lift, to lend them some money etc. – say, 'Sure. But first, we need to talk about…'

You may feel that rather than risk a row it's easier to let it go. But if you ignore the situation, nothing will change – it may even get worse. You need to have a 'problem-solving conversation'.

3. Decide what it is that you do and don't want: Set limits

You need to be clear about what is and is not acceptable to you.

By all means let your teenager blow off steam and express their anger and frustration, but you must set limits about swearing and abusive language. You may feel that any swearing is completely unacceptable or that it's OK in certain circumstances. Either way, be aware that there's a difference between swearing in general and swearing **at** someone.

Swearing in general is using extreme language and expletives in frustration or to emphasise something. Swearing **at** someone – calling them names – is verbal abuse. It's an aggressive attack directed at a person.

So 'I'm fucking pissed off with that teacher' is swearing in general. When he mumbled, 'Stupid bastard,' Jack was being verbally abusive. There's no excuse for abuse of any kind. It is not just disturbing, it's damaging. (If you swear in general or at your kids or partner, you must take responsibility and think about how you justify or change your behaviour.)

4. Start with 'I' not 'you'

A sentence that starts with the word 'you' is probably going to involve an accusation against the other person that will alert them to become defensive.

In contrast, 'I' statements will give him or her less to challenge. The other person can argue with you if you say, 'You are out of order...' but not with 'I feel upset...'

Make sure you own your feelings. Do not tell someone that they are making you feel like you do.

Simply say, 'I feel embarrassed/angry/upset when...' This also shows that you are affected by the issue and therefore need to resolve it.

5. Be prepared: Identify consequences

Although Mo will accept swearing in general, he (understandably) gets upset if Jack is abusive towards him.

It's important to calmly think of consequences before you approach someone about their hostile behaviour. Remember to think in terms of solutions and consequences, not threats and punishments. Threats and punishments usually lead to more conflict. Solutions and consequences, though, give you answers and ways forward.

Mo decided that the solution to Jack's verbal abuse was to tell him how he felt about it (upset), what he wanted (for Jack to stop swearing at him) and what the consequences would be if he didn't comply. Mo said that if he swore at him and called him names, then he wouldn't do whatever it was that he next asked from Mo, give Jack a lift to his friend's house that evening, for example.

However, one thing is crucial: whatever consequences you decide on, you have to stand firm and carry out those consequences.

Let your teenager know there **will** be consequences if he or she crosses the line. Let them know ahead of time so they won't be caught by surprise when you impose those consequences. Most importantly, **follow through**. Being consistent and sticking to what you say is the only way to show you mean business!

Of course, there may be fallout as a result. They may sulk, get angry or burst into tears. They may stop talking to you. If you stand your ground, you must accept that there may be consequences. Do not, though, let that be a reason for you to give in.

Road rage

Shona was driving through the countryside on a minor road to a meeting in a town 20 miles away. There was very little traffic but at one point, when Shona glanced in her mirror, she saw another car was suddenly driving very close to hers. Shona knew they'd reach a straight stretch in a couple of miles and thought that the other car would pass then.

When she glanced in the mirror again, the other driver was gesturing angrily at her. Shona felt a bit scared but was determined not to let the other person 'win'. However, before they did reach the straight stretch of road, the other driver overtook Shona on a bend and cut her off, forcing her to swerve onto a grass verge.

Remember, thinking of solutions, alternative courses of action and consequences gives **you** control and puts you in charge. You decide what changes you will make and what direction events are going to take if the other person doesn't cooperate.

The difficulty

To remain calm and not to engage with the other driver. Once you get angry, you are also guilty of road rage. It's dangerous to both of you as well as other drivers and will only escalate the situation.

Is it you?

Yes and no. Of course, it's not your fault if the other person drives in such a dangerous way; there's no excuse for road rage.

But, if you're determined **not** to let the other person pass, if you deliberately speed up or brake to warn the other person off, you are exacerbating the situation.

Don't give another driver another reason to get mad at you. Make sure you're concentrating properly when driving. Don't be guilty of 'lane hogging'. Don't let yourself be distracted by loud music or passengers in your car. And put your mobile phone somewhere out of sight so you're not tempted to use it while driving.

Your aim

To remain safe and calm.

What to do and say

1. Choose to be passive

Say nothing. If an angry driver yells at you or makes an angry or obscene gesture, do not respond in the same way. Keep your eyes on the road and as soon as it's safe, get out of the way of an aggressive driver. Try to make it safe for him or her to pass you: pull in, turn off or go round a roundabout twice.

Assuming that what you do want is to be safe and what you don't want is to get into a verbal or physical confrontation, put your pride in the back seat.

Why try to block that driver or confront them? You can control the situation more easily than that. How? Simply decide that you will let the other driver pass as soon as it's safe to do so. Regard it as a **positive** decision in the face of overwhelming odds that are not of your choosing and not of your making.

Do not challenge another driver by speeding up or trying to prevent him or her from getting into your lane. This will not change their attitude or behaviour. Rather, it will create an opportunity for the situation to escalate.

And don't sacrifice your own safety on the road by allowing yourself to be intimidated or break the speed limit.

Afterwards, if necessary, pull over where and when it's safe to do so, calm down then continue your journey once you're feeling steadier.

If you're being persistently harassed by the same aggressive driver, you may want to make your way to a safe, public place and call the police.

Use tact and strength

Openly hostile people are belligerent; they're ready for a confrontation, so dealing with them requires both tact and strength. On the one hand, you want to avoid provoking more anger and hostility but, on the other hand, you don't want to say or do anything that will make you appear scared, weak or a pushover.

Even if you started off feeling quite calm, when faced with an openly hostile person, you could soon feel yourself getting confused and upset, frustrated or angry.

The challenge is to manage your own heightened emotions and the other person's. Whatever the situation, there **are** ways to avoid reacting emotionally to someone else's hostility.

There are several dos and don'ts to consider:

Do

- Clarify what, exactly, the other person's problem is.
- Find out what they do and don't want.
- Set limits: what levels of open hostility are you willing and unwilling to accept?
- Acknowledge the other person's situation and feelings
- Consider compromises and solutions.
- Listen. Acknowledge the response but, if you need to, stand your ground.
- Choose a couple of assertive gestures, expressions, stances and actions to help you come across with confidence. You may not be feeling very confident but you'll certainly look it.

Don't

- Interrupt, counter-attack, get abusive, sling insults or place blame.
- Become overly defensive or counter-attack; this will only cause them to restate their case more heatedly.
- Stick around if you feel threatened or unsafe.

6
Dealing With Indirect Hostility

Dealing with somebody who is angry, upset or disappointed but unwilling or unable to be direct and honest about it is usually confusing and often infuriating.

Most of the time, it's unclear why they choose to behave in this way; their motives and intentions are hidden. If you confront a person when they're behaving in an indirectly hostile way, they will deny responsibility and turn it round on you instead.

Experience teaches most of us to avoid or minimize being around people like this. Too often, though, that difficult person is a family member or colleague, and managing the relationship by distancing yourself or cutting yourself off altogether is not really possible.

If you do have to interact with these people on a regular basis, tolerating their passive aggression will only encourage the negative behaviour to continue and intensify. The answer is to be prepared for a difficult encounter, knowing it will take a special effort to hold onto your own sense of self, stay calm to get some straight answers and clarify what's going on.

Remaining calm and composed in the face of unreasonableness will help you figure out exactly what you're dealing with. You can then plan a way forward.

Rather than try to change their attitude and behaviour, focus on how well you can manage your own. Let yourself, not the other person, be the one who sets the tone of the relationship.

Here, we look at how to assertively guide the other person into more constructive action in four different situations.

The wrong-footer

Carrie works for a small training company. She has been asked by her manager to work with Ben to write and deliver a training course for a new client. The last time Carrie worked with Ben was to deliver training to a group of medical staff. When they were planning that training, Ben was quite negative about Carrie's ideas for the training. He contributed very little himself; Carrie felt it was all left to her. On the training day, Ben didn't keep to the training plan. Instead, he added in a couple of new training activities and 'forgot' to deliver the training in the way that Carrie thought they'd agreed on. She was thrown off balance; she felt confused and her confidence was undermined.

When Carrie tried to talk to Ben about it the next day, he just shrugged and said that, on the day, he just came up with some ideas that he thought would be worth using, that he couldn't see what the problem was. Now she has to work with him again.

The difficulty

It can be incredibly frustrating when you think someone has agreed to a plan of action only to discover that you've been wrong-footed; the other person has deliberately done something you didn't expect that has put you in a difficult situation.

They are behaving in a seemingly harmless way but their insidious, underhand ways take you by surprise and, one way or another, put you at a disadvantage.

Whether it's a colleague, a friend or family member, a tradesperson – a builder, plumber, gardener – if you confront the 'wrong-footer' about their unpredictable behaviour, they will probably make excuses such as, 'I changed my mind' or claim, 'I **did** tell you', 'You didn't ask me' or 'I didn't agree to do that.'

This type of sabotage can undermine you and make it appear that it's you who doesn't know what they're doing. You are left feeling confused and frustrated.

Is it you?

It could be. When someone else does something that takes you by surprise and puts you in an embarrassing or difficult situation, it could be because you didn't give them an opportunity to express what they did or didn't want. Maybe they did try to say something but you weren't really listening. Perhaps you didn't confirm that they were happy with the plan of action and simply assumed that they had committed to it.

Your aim

To enable the other person to be clear and honest about what they do and don't want and to be clear about what you've both agreed to and then get them to commit to it.

What to do and say

If you've just been wrong-footed – if someone has just taken you by surprise and put you in a difficult situation – you may be wondering just how to respond. You may feel the urge to strike back and vent your frustration, or even become passive aggressive yourself. Neither approach is helpful, as the other person will likely respond to your overt accusations with sarcasm, denial or by putting themselves in a victim role or will respond to any passive aggressiveness on your part with even more covert hostility and then you'll just end up in an unpleasant tit for tat.

Time and energy are wasted trying to prove what was and wasn't agreed, who's right and who's wrong. If you do choose to confront the other person, avoid making accusations and statements that begin with the word 'you', because these are more likely to trigger defensiveness. Instead, use sentences that begin with 'I', followed by facts. For example, 'I was surprised that...' or 'I was disappointed when...' or 'I felt confused when...'

Rather than getting into a confrontation, reflect on what you've learnt from the experience and resolve to handle things differently next time. You can minimize the possibility of someone undermining you by taking the following steps:

1. Use active listening to find out what the other person would like to do or not do

Ask the other person for their ideas. Ask open questions such as, 'What would you like to happen?' Even if they only have a vague idea, it's a starting point, something to discuss and build on.

In the case of Carrie and Ben, Ben did actually offer a couple of ideas but Carrie wasn't listening. When you are discussing something with someone, ask yourself, 'Am I giving the other person every opportunity to give their opinion'? Often, a person will wrong-foot you because they didn't feel they had a voice or they think that they're not being listened to. You can, though, help them assert themselves, to be honest and direct about what they do or don't want.

If the other person is unsure or appears reluctant to express their ideas, offer some suggestions and ask what they think about those ideas; which ideas do they think may or may not work? What do they think would help? Try to draw them out with open-ended questions.

You can also offer them the choice to do nothing; assume they don't want to do something but struggle to be direct about it. Listen and acknowledge their response.

Having a 'let's work together' attitude goes a long way to helping the other person to assert themselves and say what they honestly feel.

2. Be prepared to negotiate and compromise

Now that you have helped the other person to assert themselves, you are in a position to respond. You may disagree with their ideas and opinions, so find common ground for a solution and try to offer an alternative that works for you and benefits the other person as well.

Using reflective listening skills, Carrie, for example, should have listened and acknowledged Ben's two ideas, suggested her own, discussed all their ideas – the pros and cons – and then negotiated on what to include and what to leave out.

3. Stand your ground

If, though, when you ask the other person what they want to see happen they are unresponsive or refuse to express an opinion, take a stand and tell them what you are going to do and what you are willing to do to move things forward.

Remain flexible: offer the other person an opportunity to express their thoughts and feelings about what you suggest but tell them that if they don't respond you'll assume they are OK with your ideas or plan of action.

4. Confirm what has been agreed

At the end of a conversation or meeting, confirm what you think has been accepted and agreed about what is going to happen next. If this is a situation at work, you can confirm the agreement in writing, in an email, for example. Keep a note of facts, issues, agreements, disagreements, timelines and deadlines.

Even with family and friends, you can send a less formal email detailing what you've both agreed. Ask the other person to reply to confirm that they are happy with what you are both going to do, but remain flexible – ask them to include any changes they may have thought of since you spoke.

5. Identify consequences

Decide what the consequences will be if the other person goes back on what was agreed and wrong-foots you again. It may or may not be appropriate to tell the other person in advance, but if you do, make sure you express your intentions in terms of consequences and not threats. Keep everything factual, not emotional.

Explaining consequences is one of the most powerful things you can use when dealing with a potential wrong-footer. Calmly articulated, consequences lower resistance and compel cooperation.

Indirect controlling

Ellie is part of a community group which is raising money to renovate the local community hall. Ellie is on the events team. They run events such as pop-up restaurants, quizzes, pantomimes and discos. Dee is responsible for the publicity. Her role is to promote events via social media and to get posters designed, printed and distributed.

Whenever Ellie or one of the events team emails her with details of an event they want promoted, Dee finds a way to resist; she stalls and is obstructive.

Dee's email responses to requests usually start with a compliment. She tells them, for example, that they're all doing a great job and are a 'fab team' but she then goes on to find a way to obstruct the team's requests.

Recent pretexts have begun with, 'That's a great idea. It would be brilliant, though if...' and 'Top idea. Only problem is...' And 'First things first – you lot are awesome ... but it will be difficult to...' and 'A fabulous idea! We just need to wait a bit in order to...'

Dee then gives a reason – or, rather, an excuse – to justify a different course of action.

She stalls and delays actions; publicity isn't forthcoming or is late and the rest of the events team often end up doing a last-minute panic job themselves.

Recently, the events team organized a Mexican Night at short notice. When Ellie emailed Dee asking for the event to be promoted, Dee's response was, 'It's a shame to have such a short lead-in time to work with – I hope we can come up with a workable solution.'

Ellie finds Dee's approach patronizing, condescending and very frustrating.

The difficulty

It's not easy to get to grips with a person like Dee – she is controlling without appearing to be. (Dee privately thinks that the events team is a bunch of amateurs; she thinks she could do better but doesn't have the time to do the publicity *and* organize events.)

When someone behaves in this way, rather than be direct and honest about what they think, they use pretexts (dishonest excuses) to conceal the true purpose or rationale behind their actions and words. Typically, they give mixed messages and are unclear about what they really mean.

Is it you?

You may feel that it is. You may feel confused and frustrated and wonder whether you are overreacting. If you have to deal with someone like Dee, it's easy to react by playing the same game: using underhand ways to get back at them. **Don't get sucked in.** There **are** constructive ways to deal with this difficult person.

Your aim

To take back control of the situation and get what you want.

What to do and say

1. Identify solutions and alternative courses of action

Ask yourself these questions:

- What do I want the other person to do or not do?
- What am I prepared to negotiate and compromise on?
- What will the solution be if the other person refuses to cooperate?

Having thought about what, exactly, you do or don't want and how far you're prepared to negotiate and compromise, you will need to decide what the solution will be if the other person digs their heels in and refuses to cooperate.

For example, before she spoke to Dee, Ellie could have thought through in advance what the solution and way forward would be if Dee looked like she might try to block Ellie's request.

Remember: it's important to think in terms of solutions, not threats. Threats raise the emotional temperature and usually lead to more conflict. Solutions, though, give you alternative ways forward if the other person won't cooperate.

Thinking of solutions and alternative courses of action gives you control and puts **you** in charge. **You** decide what changes you will make and what direction events are going to take if the other person doesn't cooperate.

Ellie has decided that if Dee won't cooperate, if she cannot commit to organizing the publicity for the Mexican Night by a particular date, the events team can organize the design and printing of the posters themselves.

2. Say what you want and don't want

State what you need. If the other person doesn't seem to be listening, or tries to sidetrack you, stick to your point. Repeat it calmly until you feel that you are being heard.

Do not back down, defend your request or counter-attack. Calmly respond to the other person in a way that both acknowledges you have listened and confirms you are standing firm.

For example, Ellie could say, 'I understand you feel it's short notice and I agree with you, it is short notice [*acknowledging what Dee said*]. We still need the posters by the end of next week though.' [*sticking to what she wants*]

3. Stand your ground or negotiate

Where possible, aim to negotiate, to find a solution that works for you and the other person as well. Ask questions to find out what, exactly, the other person is prepared to do.

For example, Ellie said to Dee: 'OK. I'll phone you on Tuesday – if by then you don't think you can get them done by the end of the week, don't worry; we'll sort out the posters ourselves. Would you be OK to Tweet about the event and post it on Facebook?'

4. What if the other person refuses to cooperate?

If the other person still appears to be procrastinating or finding excuses, don't get angry or defensive. Instead, calmly disengage yourself from the conversation.

Negative Ned

Sam's brother, Ned, has a negative approach to most things in life and sees himself as being at the mercy of other people's actions. Ned focuses on the downside of every issue.

Sam, Ned and their sister Natalie all live in London. Their mum, Pat, who was widowed a year ago, lives 100 miles away. She would like to move to London and live closer to her children and grandchildren. Whenever Sam and Natalie discuss it with Ned, he has nothing positive to contribute. He says that their mum won't like living in London, that she won't like living in a flat and that she'll expect them to call round all the time and run errands for her and so on.

If Sam or Natalie ask, 'Don't you want Mum to move closer to us and her grandchildren?' he responds with, 'I never said that,' but refuses to acknowledge anything positive about their mother moving nearer to them all.

The difficulty

Other people can be seen as drains or radiators; radiators emanate warmth and draw you towards them, whereas drains suck the life out of you. Ned is a drain.

The difficulty here is to resist being sucked in, to stay positive and take action despite the other person's negativity. A negative person's views are likely to be firmly entrenched, so it's pointless trying to argue: they'll find all sorts of reasons to back up their way of interpreting events.

Is it you?

No. Negative people get stuck in patterns of negative ways of thinking and behaving, focusing on the negative and ignoring the positive aspects of a situation. It's a habit they've developed; it's their default way of thinking. It's not surprising if you feel exasperated or drained by their negative attitude.

Your aim

To acknowledge their way of seeing things. To avoid disagreeing with them and, instead, to focus on the positive aspects of a situation.

What to do and say

1. Have positive expectations

It's easy to have negative expectations of a negative person, but it will come out in your verbal and non-verbal communication and this can just feed into the other person's negativity.

Try coming at them with the positive mindset you wish they had. It's not easy to talk naysayers out of their misery. They are usually resistant to thinking differently. The best you can aim for is to understand their perspective without endorsing it.

2. Acknowledge what the other person says

If what you hear are complaints, criticisms and negative interpretations of events, don't interrupt, defend, agree or disagree. Just listen. Acknowledge what they've said and how they feel. Remember, just reflecting the person's feelings by saying things like, 'It seems that you feel frustrated by...' can help the other person feel understood. Acknowledge their points and feelings and move on.

You can even pre-empt what they'll say by bringing up the negative aspects yourself. Then dismiss the negatives logically and direct attention to the more positive aspects of the situation.

3. Identify solutions

As negative people tend to dismiss every solution you bring up, ask them what they think may be the best solution. When Ned said, 'Someone is going to have to sort out Mum's house. She'll never be able to take all that stuff with her. I've told her hundreds of times that she should sort out all that clutter. But, of course, she never listens to me,' Natalie acknowledged what he said but focused only on what he said that was relevant – the need to sort out their mum's belongings – and she asked Ned how he thought they could tackle that.

If you listen carefully, you can often find something in what the other person says, in the same way Natalie did, that you can turn into something positive. It's hard work but it is possible.

How you ask questions and restate what the other person said is crucial. Keep your tone calm and neutral. Avoid coming across as sarcastic or hostile.

When you respond to their answer, remember to stick to the issue and not respond to their negativity. It's crucial that you avoid getting sucked into the other person's negativity – focusing on what's relevant is a way to do that.

Regardless of what they say, you can choose to declare what you are willing to do. Or you can simply get on with what you need to get done.

4. Challenge extreme terms

Often, when people are being negative, they speak in extreme terms that match their worldviews. (Ned claimed he'd told their mother 'hundreds of times' to sort through all her things.)

So, if the other person says, 'I **always** have to' or 'It **never**...' Acknowledge their view, but then present your perspective. 'I understand that it seems like it's **always** you, and yet...'

5. Take responsibility for how you feel

Don't allow guilt about wanting to avoid their negativity make you spend the next two hours listening.

You can tell the other person that their constant negativity is a drain. If you do, take responsibility for how you feel, rather than accuse them of 'making' you feel drained. Natalie or Sam could, for example, say, 'I find it difficult to remain positive when your responses are so negative. Let's talk about this another time.'

Difficult teenager

Jenny and Paul's daughter, Sophie, is 14. She has recently become very difficult. She shuts herself away in her bed-room and doesn't answer when she's called. She either

---

'forgets' to do jobs like vacuum or wash up or does them badly. Sophie often comes home later than she agreed to – she says the bus didn't turn up or she left something at a friend's and had to return to collect it. Sophie doesn't answer her phone when Jenny or Paul call her to find out where she is. Jenny and Paul nag, threaten and repeat themselves, but Sophie doesn't pay much attention to anything they say.

The difficulty

The difficulty for Jenny and Paul is getting Sophie to communicate and cooperate. Because they don't know how to negotiate and compromise, many teenagers become experts at this kind of hostile passive aggressive behaviour. They use passive resistance to gain control and get back at you. They don't want to do what their Mum and Dad say, so they pretend not to have heard you, they 'forget' what you said or they say, 'You never told me that.' They invent elaborate excuses for why they did or didn't do something.

Is it you?

Yes. When your child makes the change from childhood to adulthood, you also have to make some changes – in the way you communicate as a parent. Your teenager has got to a stage where they have their own opinions and preferences but either don't know how to negotiate and compromise or have been shut down when they do. You must both learn to negotiate and compromise; you must help your teenager shift from a position of passive aggressive resistance to one of open discussion and mutual agreements.

Your aim

To negotiate and compromise. To follow through with solutions and consequences if your teenager doesn't cooperate.

What to do and say

1. Be prepared: Identify potential solutions and consequences

If you're currently struggling to deal with a difficult teenager and there's something you want them to do, start by asking yourself:

- What do I want and not want?
- What am I prepared to compromise on and how far will I negotiate; what are my limits?
- What will the solution, way forward and consequences be if he or she refuses to cooperate?

Having thought about what, exactly, you do or don't want and how far you're prepared to negotiate and compromise, you'll need to decide what the solution will be if your teenager doesn't do what you ask.

For example, before she asked Sophie to vacuum the house, Jenny decided what the solution and consequences would be if Sophie didn't comply.

Remember, it's important to think in terms of solutions and consequences, not threats or punishments. Threats are a warning of trouble; they raise the emotional temperature and usually lead to more conflict. Solutions, though, give you alternative ways forward if the other person won't cooperate.

And instead of thinking in terms of punishments, it's far better to think in terms of logical consequences. Consequences are the natural result of the other person's action or inaction. **Consequences can lower resistance and compel cooperation.**

2. Say what you want and what you don't want

Be specific, keep it short and concise. Your point will be lost if you ramble, nag or moan. Jenny simply said, 'I'd like you to vacuum the house today.'

3. Listen and acknowledge or clarify the reply

Rather than say what they feel or think, the other person may mutter their dissent to themselves or use a non-verbal way of expressing their feelings, for example by not saying anything, giving dirty looks or rolling their eyes. Do not get drawn in!

Sophie rolled her eyes and replied that she'd homework to do in the morning and was going out with her friends in the afternoon.

Before she responded, Jenny clarified what Sophie had said, 'Are you saying you're busy all day?' She kept her voice calm and neutral. You must avoid coming across as hostile in any way.

4. Negotiate and compromise

As much as possible, aim to negotiate and compromise. Look for solutions and alternative courses of action. In this case, Jenny simply asked Sophie when would be a good time for Sophie to vacuum. Asking what works for the other person shows that you are not just making demands, that you are prepared to be flexible and that they have a choice.

Sophie's reply to Jenny's question was 'tomorrow'. Instead of insisting that Sophie comply and do the vacuuming today, Jenny compromised and negotiated. She said, 'OK. Tomorrow is fine with me, but I'd like it done in the morning. How does that sound?'

Be reasonable about the timeframe and give them choices so that they feel they have some control over what they do or don't want.

However, as a parent of three boys – all now grown up – I have to admit to a certain amount of manipulation here! I taught our sons to negotiate by asking for something to be done at an unreasonable time. For example, when they were in their early teens, if one of them – say it was Tom – was going out for the evening, I would say that he had to be in by 10 p.m. This was, in fact, an hour earlier than I did actually want him home. Tom would protest and say it wasn't fair. I would ask what time he wanted to come home and he would say, 'Midnight.' We would then quickly reach a mutually agreeable time – 11.15. Tom soon learnt this way of negotiating and compromising; it soon became second nature to him!

Often, people behave in a passive aggressive way because they don't feel they have any power or say in what does or doesn't happen. Being prepared to negotiate means that you give the other person a voice.

Also, when you negotiate and compromise, you've neither given in nor become so het up that the other person can divert the issue by accusing you of losing it.

5. Stand your ground

If you do choose to negotiate or compromise, bend as far as you can, but no further. Know what your limits are and stand your ground.

It's at this point that you should explain what the solution and consequences will be if your son or daughter doesn't cooperate. They need to take responsibility if they don't do what they agreed to.

Jenny explained that it was fine for Sophie to vacuum the next day and she'd be happy to give Sophie a lift to her friend's house at lunchtime. But that if Sophie didn't vacuum, she'd wait until it was done before she gave her a lift.

If your teenager argues, you don't need to defend yourself, argue or back down. Instead, calmly respond in a way that both acknowledges you have listened and confirms you are standing firm. For example, 'You may think I'm being unfair [*acknowledging what Sophie said*] but I still want you to vacuum this weekend. Once you've done it, I'm happy to give you a lift' [*sticking to what she wants*]. Don't get drawn into an argument – acknowledge their points and feelings and move on.

Keep consequences relevant. Don't say, 'If you don't come home on time, I'm taking your laptop away.' Do say, 'If you don't come home on time, I will need to phone your friends to find out where you are.'

And don't say, 'If you don't do your homework again, you'll lose your phone for three days.' Do say, 'If you don't do your homework, I'll need to make an appointment to see your teacher to discuss what we can do.'

The ability to assert consequences is an effective way of dealing with a passive aggressive person. Consequences give pause to a difficult person and compel them to shift from obstruction to cooperation. But you must follow through; otherwise, you'll lose all control!

Thinking of solutions, alternative courses of action and consequences gives **you** control and puts you in charge. You decide what changes you will make and what direction events are going to take if the other person doesn't cooperate.

Recognize the warning signs

When you can recognize typical passive aggressive actions, comments and behaviour for what they are – indirect, dishonest ways a person expresses what they really feel, do or don't want – then you have a head start in your dealings with them.

Some of the most common passive aggressive behaviours that you need to be aware of include sulking, stalling, 'forgetting', blaming someone or something else, ignoring, making excuses and lying. All these things are ways a person can use to indirectly control, manipulate or sabotage.

Refuse to engage

Being able to recognize passive aggressive behaviours at face value can alert you to a potential no-win power struggle. When you sense these destructive dynamics coming into play, try to prepare by telling yourself, 'They are being passive aggressive and I will not play their game,' and 'I will not yell or be sarcastic because this will only play into their hands.'

Remember, it will take a special effort to hold onto your own sense of self, stay calm and get some straight answers in order to clarify what's going on with the other person. You need to remain calm and composed so that you can assertively guide the other person into more constructive communication.

There are several dos and don'ts to consider:

Do

- Remember that people often behave in a passive aggressive way because they don't feel they have any control or a say in what does or doesn't happen.

- Assume the other person does or doesn't want to do something but struggles to say so.
- Give them a voice, enable them to assert themselves, to be honest and direct about how they feel and what they do or don't want.
- Ask the other person for their ideas. Ask open questions such as, 'What would you like to happen?' Ask them what they think would be the best solution.
- Offer suggestions and ask for their opinion.
- Compromise. Being prepared to compromise and negotiate means that you give the other person a voice.
- Confirm what you think has been agreed.
- Stand your ground. If they are unresponsive or refuse to express an opinion, take a stand and tell them what you are going to do to move things forward.
- Identify consequences (not threats). Remember, consequences lower resistance and compel cooperation.

Don't

- Get drawn into the other person's way of dealing with things; avoid using sarcasm, excuses and lies. Remain honest and calm.
- Make accusations and statements that begin with the word 'you'. Instead, use sentences that begin with 'I', followed by facts.
- Try to prove what was and wasn't agreed, who's right and who's wrong.
- Get angry or defensive. If the other person still appears to be procrastinating, blaming, finding excuses and so on, calmly disengage yourself from the conversation.

7
Dealing With Passive People

Most people would consider someone else's niceness, calmness and tolerance to be positive qualities that make interactions pleasant for everyone involved. For the most part, their passivity deflects confrontation and conflict. Well, it may be true that the meek shall inherit the earth but that doesn't make it any easier for the rest of us!

While passive people are easy-going and easy to like, they can be difficult to deal with. Rather than speak up, passives take the path of least resistance by either avoiding or accommodating people and situations.

The trick is to be assertive with these people before you become irritated and impatient with them. You are much more able to deal with a passive person when you like them and when you view them positively, rather than when you've become irritated and impatient with them!

The flaky friend

Lizzie and Sarah's children go to the same playgroup. Sarah is lovely; she's kind, gentle and calm – she and Lizzie get on very well and often arrange to do things together – coffee in the morning while the children are at school, outings in the holidays with the kids and so on.

The problem is that Sarah often pulls out of arrangements because of someone else's needs or demands. Yesterday, she cancelled a play date for their children because, she said, another mother had asked Sarah's daughter to go to her house to play with her child, Ruby. Ruby had been off school with a broken leg and was bored.

Recently, Sarah pulled out of a birthday trip that Lizzie had organized to London to see a show, with the children. Sarah explained that her mum – who is on her own – had asked to come and stay with her and that she, Sarah, couldn't say no; her mum is lonely.

When she lets Lizzie down, Sarah always apologizes and says how awful she feels about it but that she finds it difficult to say no. Lizzie is annoyed but doesn't want to drop Sarah as a friend.

The difficulty

Someone who is trying to be nice to everyone all the time often overcommits themselves because they can't say no to other people, but inevitably they end up letting someone else down. They're unavailable and unreliable.

There are times when you'll invite someone out and they'll say yes at the time of being asked. Whether they intend to come and then change their mind or find it difficult to say no directly at the time of being asked is not easy to tell.

It could be that they are indecisive, they don't really want to go but don't want to hurt your feelings or they can't say no to other demands that come up.

The question is where you draw the line. When is flakiness within a normal range and just irritating and when does it become annoying and disrespectful? There's no clear answer to that. It's something you have to judge for yourself.

Is it you?

No. It's one thing for a friend to occasionally drop out of an event, but if they do it consistently, or they repeatedly inconvenience you, then that is something to get wound up about! But if you want to keep this friend, you have to change your expectations.

Your aim

To make yourself less vulnerable to their inability to commit.

What to do and say

1. Have realistic expectations

We all have beliefs and expectations about the right and wrong way that others ought to behave towards us. When others fail to meet your expectations, you may feel disappointed, upset or resentful.

You may expect your friends, for example, to be reliable and commit to arrangements. However, if you think things can't be 'right' unless people meet your expectations, then, too often, you are going to feel disappointed, upset or angry.

Your expectations need to be realistic; they should be based on what is a real or practical way for a particular person to behave. Once you accept that your expectations are not realistic, you are in a position to do something to free yourself from being dominated by them.

Sarah has demonstrated several times that she is unreliable. Lizzie can't change this. If she still wants to be friends with Sarah, she would be better off recognizing and accepting Sarah's limits.

Having positive expectations rather than high expectations would help. High expectations lead to specific, narrow outcomes. Positive expectations, on the other hand, widen the possibilities; you simply expect and look for the positive aspects of the other person.

Imagine if, for example, Lizzie recognized that Sarah was gentle and kind with their children and calm and soothing when Lizzie was upset or had a problem. If Lizzie had positive expectations, she would simply focus on those positive aspects.

2. Be prepared: Identify potential solutions

When your expectations are more realistic – when, for example, you know that someone like Sarah is likely to let you down – you can prepare for this. You will need to decide what the solution will be to avoid being let down and disappointed if she does pull out.

Lizzie decided that next time they planned a day trip or an evening out she would not depend on Sarah turning up. Instead, she would invite other people too, so that if Sarah pulled out it would be disappointing but that Lizzie wouldn't be left high and dry.

Lizzie decided that with less important arrangements – coffee or play dates – she would always have something else to do – read a book, catch up on household chores, go to the park with her children – in case Sarah pulled out. By identifying solutions, Lizzie felt far more in control and less dependent on Sarah's ability or inability to commit.

One more thing to think about: is it the activities and outings that you make that the other person usually pulls out of? Often, you may find that when it's the other person who has made the arrangements, then the outing or social event does, in fact, go ahead.

I've got a friend like this. I have given up making arrangements to go out with her, because something always crops up for her. Instead, I wait for her to suggest something. It may be that she feels that she has to commit if it's her that has arranged for us to do something, but whatever the reason, she rarely cancels when she's arranged it!

Of course, rather than put up with a friend continually letting you down or only committing to the arrangements if they've made them, you may want to cut this person off completely. However, if you still enjoy their company and are prepared to change your expectations, you can remain friends.

A weak manager

In the last few months, Eunice's manager, Ross, distracted by personal problems, appears to have disengaged from his job. He gives little in the way of direction and support to his team. He won't confront problem colleagues or difficult clients and customers. Ross spends more time with his spreadsheets than with his staff.

In the last two weeks, Eunice's team has been having some problems with a particular project. Also, one new team member, Peri, is struggling – she doesn't take the initiative and often doesn't seem to know what she's doing.

The team also has two clients who are not forthcoming with the information they need in order to work on this particular project. Ross is indecisive about what to do. Eunice is getting frustrated, morale is low and she is also losing interest in her work.

The difficulty

A manager's job is to provide people with the direction, support and resources needed to do their jobs. But Ross is not providing this, so there's no one taking responsibility for decisions and actions. There's no one to coordinate the work, deal with problems or give feedback.

Whether you are working with a manager who has disengaged because they are stressed and burnt out or afraid of confrontation, something has got to give before the team and the work suffer irreversible damage.

Is it you?

No. Being indecisive and failing to set direction are major shortcomings for a manager. Although it's not your job to manage everyone else, rather than waste time and energy moaning about him or her, you are going to have to do something to fill the vacuum your manager has created.

By all means, talk to your manager's boss and say you're all struggling, but in the meantime, don't waste time and effort moaning and complaining about him or her – take responsibility. Focus on what it is you want and identify other ways to get the support and direction you all need.

Your aim

To get your colleagues to all work together to manage yourselves. To engage your manager in some way.

What to do and say

You have the chance to stand out by becoming an asset to your team. Try these strategies for turning unfortunate circumstances into an advantage:

1. Have realistic expectations

Once again, you need to have realistic expectations. Certainly, it's not unreasonable to expect your manager to provide direction and support but clearly that hasn't been happening for quite a while. It's obvious that you now need to change your expectations. They need to be more realistic, based on what is actually happening now.

Once you have more realistic expectations, you will be in a position to move forward. If you can recognize the positive aspects of the situation – that you can manage things yourselves – you're in a good position.

2. Identify each problem or issue and decide what you need or want

If you have a weak manager, you and your colleagues have to provide the direction, support, information and resources that you need for each other.

So, in order to start moving things forward, clearly identify what the problems with the work or project are. For Eunice and her team, one of the problems is that Peri avoids taking the initiative and doesn't appear to know what she's doing. What Eunice needs is for Peri to up her skills and be more confident.

3. Find solutions

Having identified a problem and thought about what, exactly, you need or want, you can decide what options there are for a solution.

Eunice thought through what the options were and discussed it with a couple of colleagues. They came up with a solution: to get someone to act as a mentor for Peri.

4. Use your communication skills

Just because he or she has disengaged, there's no need to cut out your manager completely. Keep lines of communication open and keep your manager informed. Eunice presented the options for dealing with Peri. She said, 'We're having problems. I've talked with Jim and Roz and here's what we think might help... What do you think?' Ask open questions.

Give him or her ideas. Follow your suggestions with asking, 'How does that sound to you? Will that be OK with you if I/we go ahead?' Give them the opportunity to provide feedback or direction; ask if there's anything else you think you should consider – anything they'd like you to include.

Request specific actions when you need support. For example, 'Could you ask HR to send us the information we need for this?' or 'Can we have a team meeting every Friday so you can give us feedback and let us know how you want to take things forward for the following week?' But limit how much you ask of them, to eliminate the disappointments.

Offer to do the work: 'Is it OK if I draft an email from you asking for the resources we need?'

As you work through this process, document everything, so that you can explain your actions if challenged.

Don't think of it as carrying your manager; you and your colleagues can either let the situation dominate your job – moaning and complaining or falling apart – or do something about it.

This will reflect well on **your** management skills, as well as help you develop good working relationships with your colleagues. It's a win–win situation!

The needy friend

Rae and Olivia are housemates at university. Since Olivia split up from her boyfriend six months ago, she has lost a lot of confidence.

Olivia doesn't see her friends or go out as often as she used to but when she does she lets Rae make the arrangements, deferring to whatever Rae suggests, saying things like, 'I don't mind' and 'It's up to you.' Before they go out, Olivia always asks what Rae thinks she should wear and once they are out – at the pub or parties – Olivia sticks by Rae's side for the evening.

Rae likes Olivia but she's finding it difficult to deal with Olivia's apathy and indecision. In fact, she's finding Olivia clingy and needy.

The difficulty

When someone is going through a difficult period in their lives, it's understandable that they feel unsure and may want to be around you more. The difficulty is to balance being understanding and supportive with making sure the other person doesn't become too dependent on you.

Is it you?

No. But you do need to know when to draw the line and be able to say no – without feeling guilty – to someone who is starting to cling to you and become needy.

Your aim

To find a balance between supporting the other person while helping them not to be too dependent on you. To help them build their confidence.

What to do and say

1. Set limits and stick to them

When you support someone by doing things like making social arrangements, reassuring and just being there for someone like Olivia, you're being a good friend. Although it's important to do this for the short term, in the long run it can create a dependent relationship: your friend's well-being will become dependent on you.

You need to set some limits. Setting limits is not always easy but it helps stop you being entangled in the other person's worries. Limits also give you the ability to step back and think about how best you can help someone else to manage their anxiety.

2. Decide what you do and don't want

In each situation, think about your own needs and what does and doesn't work for you. For example, Rae decided that she didn't want Olivia's social life to revolve exclusively round her. Rae wanted Olivia to go out with her other friends.

3. Identify a solution

Once you have decided what you do and don't want, rather than resent the fact that it's not happening you need to decide what your options are for a solution and take action.

Thinking of solutions and alternative courses of action gives **you** control and puts you in charge. You decide what changes you will make and what direction events are going to take.

Rae decided to ask Olivia's other friends to invite Rae to do things with them. Rae told Olivia's friends she was concerned about Olivia and asked that they persuade Olivia to come to the pub with them the next evening.

4. Stand firm

Learn to say no. 'No' is a powerful word but often it's hard to say, especially when it comes to friendships.

When Rae told Olivia she was going home for the weekend, Olivia asked if she could come too. It wasn't easy, but Rae had to say no. She didn't give lots of excuses or apologies. She simply explained that she wanted to spend some time on her own, with her parents and little sister.

Of course, if you choose to stand your ground, there may be fallout as a result. The other person may sulk, get angry or burst into tears. They may stop talking to you. If you stand your ground, you must accept that there may be consequences.

But you need to keep in mind that saying no to give yourself more space and to do the things you need to do without your friend is an essential part of weaning them off needing you so much. Rae didn't completely dodge her friend, but she didn't make herself so available.

5. Negotiate and compromise

Try to offer an alternative that works for you and benefits the other person as well. Rae suggested that Olivia invite some friends over for a takeaway and a film on the Sunday evening, when Rae was back from her visit home. Olivia was unsure. Rae simply said, 'I'll leave it with you.'

When you negotiate and offer to compromise, you've neither given in to the other person nor become so het up that you end up saying something you'll regret.

Remember, though, that if you do choose to negotiate or compromise, bend as far as you can, but no further. Know what your limits are and stand your ground.

6. Say how you feel

Are you spending too much time trying to help your friend through life or coming away from every encounter feeling drained and resentful?

If you choose to tell the other person how you're feeling, make sure you own your feelings. Do not tell them that they are making you feel like you do. Be honest about what's bothering you; don't lie and make up excuses.

It's not easy being told you're needy or you're draining someone. If you care about the friendship, you'll want to do it in a way that's kind.

If you think your friend needs more help than you can provide, it's best to make that clear. Rae said to Olivia, 'I'm not doing the best thing for you. You need something more than I can do. I can, though, come with you to see your GP or the university counselling service.'

Get them to participate and contribute

When you come across someone who is calm, kind and agreeable, you'll probably be pleased that you've met someone who is easy-going, easy to like and get along with. However, as you get to know them, it may become apparent that they leave all the doing and thinking to you and other people; they are indecisive or indifferent, lacking in confidence or just plain lazy.

You start to realize that it's mostly you who initiates and commits to things and it's usually you who makes the decisions and puts in most of the effort.

It's fine if you support them in the short term, but in the long run tolerating someone else's lack of participation creates an unequal relationship. Someone is going to end up feeling resentful – and that person will be you!

Remember, it's easier and kinder to deal with a passive person when you like them and when you view them positively rather when you've become annoyed and resentful towards them. Before you become too irritated and impatient with them, you need to motivate them to make a contribution, be involved and stay committed.

There are several dos and don'ts to consider:

Do

- Have positive expectations. Don't write off a passive person. Instead, expect that you **can** get some sort of contribution and commitment.
- Decide in what way you want them to be involved in something, what you need or want the other person to do.
- Get them to contribute a skill or strength or something you know they can give that's within their ability.
- Request specific actions but limit how much you ask of them, to avoid disappointment.
- Negotiate and compromise. Give the other person some ideas – follow your suggestions with 'How does that sound to you?'
- Decide what the solution will be to avoid being let down and disappointed if the other person doesn't contribute or participate.
- Recognize that if they won't contribute you must either accept it or leave them out.

Don't

- Make yourself so available. Don't put in all the time or effort.
- Let the other person be so dependent and rely on you.
- Waste time and effort moaning and complaining about their lack of participation. Instead, focus on what it is you want and find other ways to get what you need.
- Give in. Learn to say no and stick to it if the other person would rather let you do it all.

PART THREE
When All Else Fails

8
Dealing With Impossible People

Some people are more than difficult. They're impossible. The only way to deal with an impossible person is to remove yourself from them; to let them go and walk away. Of course, this is easier said than done. You'll need to think through the pros and cons for eliminating someone from your life; you'll need to consider what you have to lose and what you have to gain by letting them go and walking away.

But before we look at how to do that, let's look first at what sort of person is impossible. Quite simply, if you **think** you are dealing with an impossible person, you're probably right. They may be possible for other people, but for you they're impossible to deal with.

Below are some impossible types – people who, for most of us, are impossible.

Critical, impossible-to-please impossible people

When someone is being critical it's because they've got a problem – a situation that needs a solution. Their problem is that they can't accept you for who you are and the way

165

you are. Their solution? To get you to change, to make it your problem.

They want you to adopt their values, beliefs and ways of doing things. They never hesitate to let you know, in totally inappropriate ways, that you just don't measure up. They're impossible to please; whatever you do, it will never be good enough. They'll always insist that you could do better.

It could be a parent or in-law, a sibling, your adult son or daughter, a friend, colleague or manager. Whoever it is, they respond with criticism and judgement instead of pleasure or approval, whatever you do. They respond with criticism and judgement when you make a mistake. They often label you in an unfair way – saying you're 'clumsy', or 'not very clever', 'hopeless', 'selfish', 'lacking ambition' and so on.

Their criticisms and judgement can seriously undermine your self-confidence. You may start to believe there is something wrong with you and internalize their critical voice inside your head. If you let their criticisms and demands define you, these people will steal your life from you; their fiction will become your life story.

If you can't (or won't) cut them out of your life, you need to know that any time you spend trying to argue with them and convince them of the person you really are will be wasted.

If you can't (or won't) cut them out of your life, minimize the amount of time you spend with them. Tell them as little about yourself as you can. Don't seek their approval or give them any excuse to disapprove. Don't say anything that will give them the opportunity to dump their negative opinions and judgements on you. Only tell them what you think they absolutely need to know.

When you ignore their opinions and decide to be who you are, instead of who they want you to be, you open yourself up to being the person you want to be and on your own terms.

Identifying your values can help here (see Chapter 2). If what the other person wants you to be is at odds with your values, then you are never going to feel right trying to please them and be who they want you to be. When you are trying to behave in ways that contradict your values, you are not being true to yourself.

What does being 'true to yourself' really mean, though? It means being true to what's important to you – what you value – not what's important to someone else and what they think is important for you. Being true to yourself means following what you believe over what other people want you to do or be.

There's more to you than what the critical, impossible-to-please person sees, so keep in mind that what you're capable of is not the result of what they think. Look beyond their judgements and limiting criticisms and find the courage to be yourself. Your real value is in who you are, not who you aren't!

You can't control what others think about you, so leave them to their own judgements. They're going to find fault whatever you do. Let people like you or love you for who you are and not for who they want you to be. Or let **them** walk away!

Persistently negative impossible people

Much like the critical, impossible-to-please person, the persistently negative person has the ability to change your mood in an instant.

They constantly moan and complain about their life: their job, the weather, their family, friends and neighbours, where they live and so on. They're negative about where they've been and what they've done, where they are now and what they're doing now. They're negative about where they're going and what they'll be doing. They don't have a good word to say about anyone or anything.

If you ask them about a happy event – a meal out, their holiday or their sister's wedding, for example – they can only tell you about the negative aspects: what they didn't like, what went wrong and so on. They are so entrenched in seeing the negative side of things that they leave no room for positive things to happen.

Persistently negative people drain the life out of you. If you can't, or won't, cut them out of your life then at least cut down the time you spend with them. And when you are with them, avoid correcting their negative views because they'll only find a way to contradict your positive interpretations. Instead, say, 'Mmm', 'Oh' and 'I see' to acknowledge what they say without agreeing or challenging them.

Saying any more than the bare minimum will just add fuel to the fire.

Drama queens

Do you know someone who reacts to events with excessive emotion and behaves in theatrical, attention-grabbing ways? Do they make a big deal out of everything? In a situation that you'd score a 3 or 4 on the drama scale, do they take it up to a 10? Yes? Then you've got a drama queen on your hands!

They're the people who blow things out of all proportion. They manage to turn ordinary problems into catastrophes, but unless they're living in a war zone, the chances are that a lot of this drama is self-created.

Drama queens enjoy being the centre of attention. In fact, if they have to manufacture a scene to focus the spotlight on them, it's not a problem.

A drama queen could be the friend you're at the coffee shop with who doesn't get the right coffee and is rude and obnoxious to the person serving him. He may even drag the other customers into the situation. Or it could be the person who blows every argument with her partner or colleague out of all proportion and then spends ages telling you about it – exaggerating every detail. Drama queens are often experts at seeing themselves as the victim, as badly wronged and as deserving a lot better than what they're getting.

They have no sense of proportion. Small things like wine being spilt on their shoes, or someone inadvertently ignoring them, are viewed as disasters. There are no minor mishaps in the drama queen's world!

It's always about them – they have little time to hear about what's happening in your life. And when they do, they either turn it into a drama or they top it with an even more dramatic story of their own.

They will cast you into their dramas and if you take a side you will simply add more drama to the whole situation. You'll find yourself being sucked into their life of conflict and opposition.

If you can't, or won't, cut them out of your life, minimize the amount of time you spend with them. And when you do spend time listening to their dramas, use reflective listening skills. Don't offer your opinions. Don't get involved in their drama. Stay out of it! Simply acknowledge what they say with an 'Mmm', 'Oh' and 'I see'. Once again, saying any more than the bare minimum will just add fuel to the fire.

Self-centred impossible people

Closely related to the drama queen are their quieter, self-centred cousins. They don't particularly dramatize or exaggerate but they do routinely prioritize talking about their own feelings, situations and needs over and above yours.

If you try to talk about something to do with yourself, they steer the conversation back to themselves: their job, their health, partner, kids, work and social life. They're not interested in your thoughts and feelings.

We're not talking here about people who are interested only in themselves some of the time – we're talking about people who are only concerned with talking about themselves all the time. They are so self-absorbed that there's absolutely no room for you.

What stronger message do you need? There's no room for you. Leave right now!

Bullies

If someone is persistently badgering, dominating or intimidating you, you're being bullied. If someone is continually coercing and threatening you, criticizing or humiliating you, tyrannizing you or making abusive remarks and insulting you, you're being bullied.

Bullying can occur to your face or behind your back. Direct, overt bullying is obvious and aggressive. Indirect bullying is more underhand and less detectable. Bullying can happen face to face, by phone, text or social media.

Bullies seem to know exactly how to get at you. Sometimes you may wonder whether they actually enjoy causing so much distress. You're right: they probably do enjoy it.

How come? Well, for most of us, when we see someone else is upset or in pain we feel sympathy for the other person; we recognize the other person is hurt or upset and we feel compassion for them.

However, bullies don't interpret other people's painful emotions as a bad thing. Not only do they not care, they actually like it.

If you're being bullied you may well feel very upset, anxious, frightened, ashamed or embarrassed. You may feel angry and frustrated. You mustn't try to please, pacify or ingratiate yourself with them, but you **must** do something. The bully will not go away.

Staying silent and telling no one will only isolate you while at the same time empowering the bully, so you must get help and support.

If you feel there is no one to talk to, don't suffer in silence; there is help out there. There are organizations that specialize in supporting anyone who is being bullied. Do visit any of these websites for support and information:

- http://www.bullying.co.uk/
- https://www.gov.uk/workplace-bullying-and-harassment
- http://www.nspcc.org.uk
- http://www.childline.org.uk.

If you're being bullied, you'll probably be feeling that there's no respite and no release from the stress that they're causing you. Unfortunately, bullies are compulsive in their behaviour; once they start on their target, they won't let go. The answer? Leave. Leave the job, the relationship or the social media account.

Walking away is the best thing to do, for in doing so **you** regain control. You take away the opportunity for the bully to behave like this towards you.

Bullies are clever, but you can be clever too. You do have a choice about how to respond. Simply ask yourself what's most important. Is it that you don't want to let the bully 'win'? Is that the most important issue?

Rather than think in terms of one of you winning or losing, isn't it better to think about keeping yourself safe and sane?

Sure, it can be difficult to walk away from a job or a relationship. But know this: the energy that's draining out of you as a result of being bullied can – if you're being bullied at work, for example – be used to get a new job or – if you're being bullied in a relationship or by a housemate or a neighbour – that energy can be used to find somewhere else to live. And if you're being bullied by email, phone or via social media, close the account. You can always get a new one.

Being bullied and trying to manage being bullied is highly stressful. You have little or no control.

Sure, you may have to walk away from a good job and financial stability, but focus on the positive: you've left the bully behind. Once you leave the bully, you can put your energy into finding a new job or somewhere to live instead of spending your energy trying to please, pacify or avoid the bully.

And if you do want to think in terms of who's won and who's lost, know that if you take control and walk away YOU have won.

You can manage to find a new job or somewhere else to live. What you can't manage is the bully. So refuse to allow your life to be wrecked and get out!

Is it you?

All the impossible types described here – the bullies, the drama queens and so on – are just a few examples of impossible people. No doubt you can think of someone who is impossible in other ways. Whoever they are, they all have one thing in common: you never look forward to seeing them. To one extent or another, the thought of spending any time with these people makes your heart sink.

It's not you. It's them. Or is it? Is there any way that it could be you?

It may be that you are actually enabling someone else's impossible behaviour. In psychology and counselling, the word 'enabling' is used to describe a situation where one person responds, often with good intentions, to another in a way that perpetuates and even exacerbates another person's (often destructive) behaviour.

The enabler may do this by rescuing them from their self-imposed predicaments. For example, with their teenager who always loses their phone, the parent buys them a new one each time. Or the husband who loses his job **again** and his wife does overtime or takes on a second job to compensate.

When you enable someone else's behaviour, you take responsibility or make accommodations for the other person's harmful conduct. You may bear their negative consequences for them, with the result that the person doesn't have to and so is unaware of the harm they do and the need to change.

With the impossible people we're looking at here – a critical parent or partner, for example – if you are constantly striving to meet their expectations and seek their approval, you are enabling their critical behaviour.

And, if you try to oppose or appease a bully, you are enabling them by creating conditions that allow the bully to continue their behaviour. By opposing and challenging them, they increase their hostility. By trying to pacify them, you will only be increasing their ability to humiliate you.

Although you are not to blame for their behaviour, you are responding in such a way that you are supporting their behaviour. If, on the other hand, you walk away, you take away the enabling conditions.

How to deal with impossible people

Impossible people are called 'impossible' for a reason. If you try to talk to them about their impossible behaviour, the chances are that you'll end up being blamed for everything: **you** are the impossible person and it's unbelievable that you think it's **them**!

Maintaining a relationship with an impossible person is very difficult, if not impossible. Why is it, though, that often, despite the problems a relationship with an impossible person brings you, you push on and hope that things will get better between you?

There are several reasons why you may find it hard to let them go and walk away.

Perhaps you're scared of change and can't see an alternative way forward. Often, it's difficult to walk away from an impossible person if it could mean a big change in your life. It may be that cutting them out of your life would mean leaving your job or where you live and you worry that you will never get another job or place to live.

Another reason you may find it hard to cut someone out of your life is that you don't want to admit to yourself or others that you were wrong to have put up with an impossible person for so long. You tell yourself that you're so used to them you may as well carry on seeing them. Perhaps your family and friends told you that your partner, for example, was no good for you, or that your neighbour was intolerable – but you said that you could handle him or her and that the situation would eventually improve.

Maybe you're thinking about sunk costs: the time, effort and love you've put into the relationship or the situation. But sunk costs can fool you into sticking with something you would be better off ending; you continue to put more time, effort or money into someone or something even though it's plainly not doing you any good.

Perhaps you're finding it difficult to walk away from someone because you don't want to end up feeling guilty for cutting them out of your life. You don't want to feel that you've 'wronged' the other person.

Being scared of change, not wanting to admit to mistakes and wanting to avoid feeling guilty are all obstacles in the way of walking away from an impossible person. The good news is that you can get round these obstacles. You just need to change your mindset – to prepare yourself emotionally and mentally to cut an impossible person out physically.

So yes, it can be difficult to walk away from someone if it means a change in your situation. But think of it like this: the time and effort you waste trying to deal with an impossible person can be used to manage the change in your situation.

And, if you feel that it may well have been a mistake to be around an impossible person for so long, but you struggle to face up to that, just tell yourself that you did well at the time because you were at least trying to do **something** good – even if what you were doing was just trying to tolerate the impossible person. You can always draw something good out. At the very least, you'll have learnt something about yourself and your abilities to manage an impossible person in the future.

Just know that whether you've put up with it for a month, a year or even half a lifetime, you shouldn't carry on letting yourself be miserable because you feel all that past misery would be wasted otherwise.

Finally, if the thought of having to cope with feeling guilty is stopping you from walking away, you need to understand what guilt is: guilt is a feeling that you have done something wrong.

Instead of feeling that you are doing something wrong, recognize that you are doing something right. You are protecting yourself – your time, energy, spirit and sanity. Letting go of an impossible person doesn't mean you hate them or that you wish them harm; it just means you care about your own well-being.

Deciding to cut someone out of your life is for your own good – not theirs. You're responsible for your own feelings, not theirs. So any time you feel guilty, remind yourself of the ways in which they're impossible. And then you have your reason not to feel you've done anything wrong.

Let them go and move on by focusing on what you have to gain

The best way to move on – to get past the fear of change, the guilt, the sunk costs or admitting your relationship is a mistake – is to think about what you have to gain rather than what you have to lose by pulling out.

Whatever the reason is that you're holding onto still seeing this person, ask yourself why: is it because you really will gain something or because you don't want to lose the time, energy or money you've already invested?

But if you walk away now, although it will take time to adjust, focus on the fact that you will be free to meet people who will appreciate you. You will have more time for yourself, friends and new interests, fewer arguments, less anxiety and stress and more control over your life. So focus on what you have to gain and move forward!

Turn your face to the sun and the shadows fall behind you.
Maori proverb

If you think about what you have to gain in the future then, in your mind, you've already left the relationship. The only thing left to do is to allow the physical reality to reflect that fact.

In Chapter 4, you will have read about how to be assertive with other people. When it comes to cutting out impossible people, you need to be assertive with yourself; you need to decide how you feel and what exactly you do or don't want. (Use your values to help guide you.) The impossible person is not going to change and they are unlikely to go away. So you will need to identify the solution, which is for you to walk away and stand firm. Focusing on what you have to gain by cutting out the impossible person will help you with this.

Focusing on what you have to gain

Sam and Ginny, for example, had known each other since school days; they'd shared a flat when they left home and travelled around Europe and Asia together. They each went on to marry and have children and lived just 30 miles from each other. They no longer had any mutual friends but kept up with each other by email and meeting for lunch and days out every now and again.

In the last couple of years, Sam was finding Ginny draining. Ginny was incredibly negative, dull and boring. Everything centred around Ginny talking about her life – she never asked Sam about hers. She was sensitive too – when Ginny emailed a photo of her teenage daughters, Lila and Daisy, to Sam, Sam replied, 'Lovely photo... I see Lila's lost a lot of weight!'

Unknown to Sam, Ginny's daughter had an undiagnosed eating disorder. But Ginny emailed back, 'It was unnecessary for you to say that – we're very worried about Lila and I don't need comments like that.'

This was the last straw. Other people may not have found Ginny impossible, but Sam did. But then she thought about the history they shared and how guilty she'd feel if she didn't see Ginny any more. She talked to her partner, Nat. Nat asked Sam how, in the last couple of years, she felt at the thought of seeing Ginny. Sam recognized that, unlike meeting up with other friends whom she looked forward to seeing, Sam's heart sank – she actually felt depressed each time she thought about meeting up with Ginny. 'Well,' said Nat. 'How much worse do you want to feel before you stop seeing Ginny? How much better will you feel when you know you've decided not to see her again?'

This was the prompt that Sam needed. She decided what she **didn't** want was to feel dread at seeing Ginny. What she **did** want was to see friends she felt good about. Sam recognized that she and Ginny had some very good times in the past – nothing could devalue that – but it was time to let them go and move on.

Sam decided to use what her partner Nat called the 'stop calling and drift' method; she wouldn't confront Ginny and tell her that she no longer wanted to be friends. It might be true, but Sam felt it wasn't necessary or kind. Instead, she quietly withdrew. She started by making excuses for not meeting up, then as the months went by she told Ginny that she had a lot on and would contact Ginny when she was more free. But Sam never did call Ginny.

Sometimes, though, an impossible person all but forces a clean break. This means that either you have to ignore them and not respond to any communication from them or you actually have to let them know that you don't want to see them any more.

Making a clean break

Naomi, for example, had a friend called Carla. They'd been close since they were both divorced, two years previously. At one point, Naomi started to feel overwhelmed by Carla's neediness – Carla almost acted as if Naomi belonged to her; she became jealous and resentful if Naomi socialized without her. Naomi tried to encourage Carla to build her own social life but Carla wouldn't listen. Naomi felt suffocated. She wanted out. She phoned Carla and said she didn't want to be friends any more.

It might not have been the kindest thing to do, but for Naomi it was necessary and true. Carla was angry and reacted by accusing Naomi of being selfish and uncaring. Naomi said nothing.

Even though it was difficult, Naomi felt relieved; she felt a great weight had been lifted.

Of course, any meaningful relationship is bound to have difficulties but if you can talk about it as things come up – if you can communicate and be assertive – there's a good chance that issues will be resolved and you'll move on together.

However, if someone is truly wearing you down or you feel your relationship is entirely one-sided, don't leave yourself in a position that compromises your well-being. Remember, letting go of an impossible person doesn't mean you hate them or that you wish them harm; it just means you care about your own well-being. Deciding to cut someone out of your life is for your own good, not theirs.

Impossible people

You will probably have realized by now that you cannot deal with impossible people the same way you deal with everyone else. Maintaining a relationship with an impossible person is... impossible.

More than likely, sooner or later, you and the impossible person will part ways, whether they are a friend, a family member, a parent or even a spouse, the time to leave will eventually come.

There are several dos and don'ts to consider:

Do

* Recognize that some impossible people are impossible to please: whatever you do, it will never be good enough.
* See beyond their judgements and criticisms and find the courage to be yourself. Your real value is in who you are, not who you aren't!
* Recognize that if you can't cut them out of your life you can cut down the amount of time you spend with them.
* Know that if you do spend time with them you should avoid correcting their views and opinions. Instead, say, 'Mmm', 'Oh' and 'I see' to acknowledge what they say without agreeing with or challenging them.
* Let them go and move on by focusing on what you have to gain: more time for yourself, new interests, fewer arguments, less anxiety and stress. More time for other, less difficult people.
* Remember that walking away is the best thing to do, for in doing so you regain control. You take away the opportunity for someone to be impossible to you.

Don't

* Compromise your values and who you are.
* Enable the other person's impossible behaviour; don't take responsibility or make accommodations for them.

- Give them information that they can use against you. Don't say anything that will give them the opportunity to dump their negative opinions and judgements on you.
- Strive to meet their expectations, seek their approval or give them any excuse to disapprove.
- Try to control what they think about you; leave them to their own judgements. They're going to find fault whatever you do.
- Put up with them and carry on being miserable just because you've already put up with them for a month, a year or even half a lifetime.
- Dwell on what you have to lose by cutting them out; focus on what you have to gain.
- Think letting go means you hate them or wish them harm. Remember, cutting someone out of your life is for your own good, not theirs.
- Think in terms of one of you winning or losing. Instead, think about keeping yourself safe and sane.

Conclusion

Positive people

Having read this book, you'll be clearer about what makes for difficult and impossible people. You'll know that they are the ones who bring you down with their negativity, criticisms or anger. They're often self-centred and uncooperative. They're irritating, frustrating and often infuriating.

You'll know ways to identify their motives and true intentions. You will have learnt ways to deal with other people calmly, directly and honestly using assertiveness skills and techniques. You'll have strategies to stand up to others and feel more confident about knowing when to walk away.

If you do choose to spend less time with difficult and impossible people or cut them out completely, you will have more room and more time for positive people in your life; people who you feel good being around; people who you can be yourself with.

It's not difficult to spot positive people. Think about people in your life and ask yourself these questions:

- What kinds of feelings does this person evoke?
- How would I describe this person in three to five words?
- Do I like who I am when I am around this person?

A positive person could be the person who supports you when you're down and is fun when you're up. It could be someone who provides wisdom and advice when you're lost.

A positive person could be someone who sees your strengths even when you don't. It could be someone who has compassion towards themselves and others; they are open minded and willing to learn from their own mistakes.

It could be someone you know who is courageous about following their dreams; he or she seeks to be authentic and believes in themselves. They inspire you.

They are the ones worth keeping in your life. Everyone else is just passing through.

Which people come to mind from the statements below?

- Someone I can call on in a crisis.
- Someone who makes me feel good about myself.
- Someone I can totally be myself with.
- Someone who values my opinion.
- Someone who tells me how well I am doing.
- Someone I can talk to if I am worried.
- Someone who really makes me stop and think about what I am doing.
- Someone who makes me laugh.
- Someone who introduces me to new ideas, interests or new people.

You may have a different person or a number of people for each situation. Or the same one or two people may feature on the list.

People sometimes tell me that they don't have anyone in their lives who can inspire them to reach greater heights, that they don't have anyone in their lives who is fun or who can support them in difficult times.

Yes they do. So do you.

Be creative in your thinking. The positive people on your list do not just have to be friends or family; they could be colleagues or neighbours. Maybe the person who makes you laugh is a stand-up comedian on the TV. The person who you can turn to in a crisis may be a listener from the Samaritans or someone in a support group, a financial adviser or your GP. The person who inspires you could be someone you have read about who has overcome adversity.

Get in the habit of reading about people – ordinary people or famous people – who inspire you. You need positive role models in your life. But don't just read about positive people. Search them out. Search out people who have the same interests as you.

If you don't have anyone on your list who introduces you to new ideas, interests or new people, join an adult education class or a special interest group. Get together with like-minded people to develop an interest – singing, tennis, walking, local history, for example – or promote a cause – raising money for cancer research, renovating a local building, for example.

And if you want more positive people in your life, start by being more positive yourself.

Doing something to benefit someone else can make you and the person you are helping feel good. This can create a bond between you, help you to develop empathy and bring a fresh perspective to your own life and circumstances.

It's never been easier, thanks to new technologies – the Internet and social networking sites – to find other, positive people.

You become like the company you keep. So choose carefully. As Oprah Winfrey has said, 'Surround yourself only with people who are going to lift you higher.'

About the Author

Gill Hasson is a teacher, trainer and writer. She has 20 years' experience in personal development. Her expertise is in the areas of confidence and self-esteem, communication skills, assertiveness and resilience.

Gill delivers teaching and training for education organizations, voluntary and business organizations and the public sector.

Her writing includes books on the subjects of resilience, communication skills, assertiveness, mindfulness and emotional intelligence.

Gill's particular interest and motivation is in helping people to realize their potential, to live their best life! You can contact Gill via her website www.makingsenseof.com or email her at gillhasson@btinternet.com.

Acknowledgements

Thanks to my editors Jonathan Shipley and Jenny Ng.

Index

Index

Index

Index